Introducing You to Yourself

Your Journey to Self-Clarity Starts Here...'

Karthik Narayana Reddy

Clever Fox
PUBLISHING

Chennai • Bangalore

CLEVER FOX PUBLISHING
Chennai, India

Published by CLEVER FOX PUBLISHING 2023
Copyright © Karthik Narayana Reddy 2023

CONTENTS

PREFACE

- Have you ever felt like you don't love your life anymore?
- Have you ever thought about how much you neglect caring about yourself in pursuit of caring for others?
- Have you ever realised that the World around you is nothing more than a reflection of your thoughts and actions?

Now, thoughts like this in recent times made me want to develop myself on a personal level. And thanks to COVID, I decided to invest on my Personal Growth through one of the coaching courses by Vikram Dhar in early 2021.

Since everything was accessible from home and was online, it felt a lot more convenient and hence started exploring a lot more options which I felt could help in my own Personal Development.

Then decided to expand my network to reach out to new people, got into BNI and then into ILH and finally now working with my coach Thaddeus Lawrence on Vertical Coaching (as he would call it) and the importance of Human Connections (again his words), all as a part of my Personal Development.

That made me realise, there are many people out there who need to work on caring for themselves but don't, due a their own reasons.

So, I decided bring together my expertise from all these years of work in Fingerprint Analysis and this newfound key to Personal Development through Coaching, to identify the key areas or aspects of life that we need to work on, to enhance our 'Understanding of Self'.

This book is years of my work and understanding of self clarity that have been concise to be simple enough so that the concepts of Self Clarity can be understood rather easily. There are activities of Self Assessment after each chapter which will help you give some time with yourself and your thoughts so that you get your daily dose of self-care that we all so badly need.

Your Life is in Your Hands, quite literally too. Build Your World around Your Understanding of Self rather than trying to rule someone else's World.

I came across a saying in my schooling years which said, "Knowledge is Power" and that kind of got stuck in my head for as long as I can remember, didn't really know why. But it was not until a few years ago that I realised, "Knowledge of Self is the Most Powerful".

And here's my attempt to apply that 'Knowledge' to help you Understand Yourself Better.

INTRODUCTION

- It was about 10 years ago that I got introduced to the concept of Dermatoglyphics, which in common terms is the study of Fingerprint Patterns and its Ridges.
- It was by total accident that I landed up in one of the stalls who were already analysing fingerprints of people and were counselling them based on it.
- It was a 'School Expo' in 2012, that was held in Palace Grounds of my city, Bengaluru that I came across this stall. I had been there with one of my friends on a totally different purpose, to start a Pre-school.

Ironically, I ended up giving my fingerprints and paying an advance amount to get my counselling done based on my finger-prints.

About 2-weeks later I get a call saying my 'Report' is ready and I can come for counselling. Those were well before COVID days, so pretty much everything happened offline. So we decided to meet in one of the cafes to have this session for me and by the time I reached, they were already there, expecting me.

Now, the intriguing part of all this was yet to come. Here's a person sitting across the table, looking at his laptop and telling me about myself. And he was pretty accurate to most part. So, now I wanted to know more about

- what was happening?
- how is he doing this?
- how does he know what I am capable of?

my thought process, my strengths and weaknesses.

Turns out, it was an art of learning how to decode your fingerprints and put it in a meaningful way to help us understand ourselves better. The emphasis was on 'Natural Abilities, Natural Traits' that we need to identify in each one of us to know ourselves better and subsequently live a more satisfied and happier life.

That made me think of all the wrong choices I had made till then due to the lack of Awareness, especially choosing my Career, which I have mentioned in detail in one of the sections of this book.

But the thought that I immediately got was that we can revolutionise the education sector with this tool.

Ya, I know, immature thoughts, immature excitement. Who are we kidding. But then, when I got deeper into the subject of Dermatoglyphics, the clearer it became on how powerful this tool could be if used in the right way.

Through the course of these last few years, I have been learning so much about myself, and have been helping a lot of people who came my way or crossed paths with me in this journey of wanting to know more about themselves. Though my work of helping people Understand Themselves Better is extremely satisfying and helping me grow as a person too, I am amazed about how little people have heard about this amazing tool.

The purpose of writing this book is not to sell the tool but to introduce those common aspects in your life which need to be understood better to make life more meaningful.

Identifying Your Abilities, Traits, Interests, Strengths & Limitations just by analysing your fingerprints, now that's a hook that I would never let go off. And that was my first step towards understanding myself better.

Through this book, I intend to impact a lot more people in realising the importance of Self Awareness or Self Clarity as I would call it, with or without the tool of Fingerprint Analysis.

As you read on you'll find different parameters that you need to have an understanding of, to start your journey of Self Clarity.

You'll also find some activities in each chapter, which will help you assess your understanding of self, be more conscious and aware of what you do and why you do things.

With that said, let's and explore what my first book has in store to offer you, shall we?

ARE YOU READY TO FALL IN LOVE WITH YOUR LIFE, ALL OVER AGAIN?

If YES, then with no further ado, let's dive right in.

Part 1

MY INTRODUCTION TO YOU
From 'My Story' to 'A Blueprint to Your Self Clarity'

Here's what you'll find in this Part of the Book

Section 1: My Story

Section 2: Your Own Multiverse of Madness

Section 3: The Journey of Self Clarity

Section 4: Are You Ready for a Journey of Your Lifetime?

Section 5: A Blueprint to Your Self-clarity

SECTION 1

My Story

It's been a little over 12 years since I completed my Engineering and to date, I am not quite sure about 'WHY' I did it.

Now that I have your attention, let's talk.

I know it sounds stupid to admit that my career choice was a joke on the very first page of my very first book but hey, that's where we are. To be honest, so was the decision-making process at the time. Stupid.

So, let me start with my story of choosing Engineering for my graduate studies and a few choices which led to that decision in the first place.

Engineering happened to me more by chance than by choice. Everything was all good and rosy till my schooling was complete but what came next was where things started to go wrong.

There was a very popular theory that invisibly prevailed everywhere around our education system during my time of studying. I am pretty sure some of it still exists and there are many students still getting into the trap of that same theory even today.

Do you want to know what that theory was? Would you like to take a guess?

BEHOLD, presenting to you, The Career Choosing Theory of a Lifetime. Well, here it goes, at your own risk.

- If you score 85% or above in your 10th grade, you inevitable choose SCIENCE as your stream for your Pre-university course (or 11th grade as it is called these days)
- Your score in 10th is anywhere between 65% to 85%, and you are automatically pushed into the COMMERCE stream.
- Less than 65%, ARTS.

And this theory held good for almost 80% of the students who had to make career choices in my time. If you were in the other 20%, LUCKY YOU..!

Do you want to know what's worse?

According to some recent surveys including the one conducted by EdTech Reviews, over 80% of students today have no idea about the career path to choose. Seems like they are also as confused as I was 16 years ago, if not even worse.

Now is that not alarming enough yet, in the year 2022?

Can we not do anything about it?

At my time, neither did I have the awareness nor the confidence to challenge or even question this famous Theory of Careers that so royally prevailed among us. It was much later in my life that I realised, my abilities and interests are inclined towards the SOCIAL & ARTISTIC niches and not towards Science & Technology.

And guess what, all those who take up Science in their Pre-university Course (or 11th grade) are bound to choose either Medicine or Engineering as their professional course, in most cases.

Yeah, now you know why I called Engineering in my life to be more a chance and not a choice. Just take a moment here to see if you could relate to my story of choosing a career path to something that you might have faced in your life too.

Has something similar happened to you too?

Or maybe you know someone who has been a product of mind-blowing theories like this?

Our system of education I tell you. Classic.

Anyway, the only sensible reasoning that I could deduce for the path that I took all those years ago or that the current flock of students are still falling into today, is the LACK OF AWARENESS. The LACK of 'Clarity and Direction'. Not just in terms of choosing careers but in making any kind of decision, especially during the crucial stages of life.

And that's a major problem which everyone tends to acknowledge but does very little to address it. Don't you think so?

Have you ever experienced situations in your life where you had to choose something with whatever limited awareness you had at the time and regretted it later? I am sure you would come up with a list of things to talk about.

We've all been there in our lives, in our own ways, haven't we?

And we often tend to blame the situations and circumstances that life throws at us, for us to struggle. Me included, been there, done that.

I've heard a saying from a wise person, which goes something like, 'Schools and colleges teach you the lessons first and then test you, but Life has its own way. Life tests you first and then teaches you the necessary lessons.' Beautiful isn't it?

This saying, kind of hit me hard when I started making the wrong decisions, not knowing that they were wrong at the time of deciding.

But what's life if you don't learn from your experiences and get better equipped to face the next day, right?

Anyway, let's focus on that wise saying for a bit.

It says, Life tests you first and then teaches you lessons. Very True, to an extent.

If you know to read between the lines, it doesn't say that you can't prepare for the tests that Life throws at you.

Confused?

Let me give you an example.

Let us say, you would have to face around 1000 unfamiliar situations in the next 10 years, that's 100 different unfamiliar situations in a year, about 2 of them every week.

That's a decent assumption to make, I suppose.

These unfamiliar situations are the tests of life that you face, some of them might be easier and some difficult. You might be able to navigate through some and there would be some situations which can break you down.

Irrespective of all the unfamiliar situations that you might have to face in your life, there is one factor that always remains common. Do you know what that is?

It is YOU..!

Yes, you heard it right, the only common factor in all the unfamiliar situations that you face in your life is undoubtedly YOU.

Now, here's a question for you,

'Is it better to put your efforts and energies to understand and analyse the common factor of unfamiliar situations (YOU)?'

OR

'Is it wise to anticipate and analyse all possible unfamiliar situations that you might or might not face in your life?'

What do you think is a more sensible thing to do?

Both ways you try and prepare to face the unknown, but which part of the question do you think is under your control?

Is it not wise to work on understanding yourself better? Understand your strengths & limitations better?

Isn't that something that is in your control?

Working on the common factor of all the situations, which is YOU, is how you prepare yourself to take on the challenges that life throws at you. It is never the other way around. Learn from your life experiences and get better equipped to face the next challenge.

Focus on what makes you better instead of feeling helpless or victimised for what you have to go through in your life.

Is that compelling enough an argument for you to agree that 'Understanding of Self' or 'Self-clarity' is more important than we actually give it credit for? I guess that is some food for thought after all.

Read on to get introduced to **'Your Own Multiverse of Madness'**.

Your Own Multiverse of Madness

Decision-making in your life is like choosing the option which you feel is the most accurate at the time of making it. The questions that you face in those unfamiliar territories often come with multiple choices, which you can choose from. But the choice you make decides the path to your next question.

Something similar to the MCU's concept of MULTIVERSE. A different choice made at a given point in time leads you into a totally different timeline, a totally different universe.

We all have our 'What If..?' moments, don't we?

Ok now that we have established I follow Marvel Comics series, let's get back to the multiverse of OUR own madness, shall we?

I know, there'll always remain a thought on our minds that 'If I had chosen the other option available at the time, maybe my life would have been different, maybe better'. Because the grass is always greener on the other side, you see.

But the truth is, we would never know if it would have turned out better or worse because that's not the option we chose.

I believe, that the choices we make, define the timelines of our lives, and the timelines of our Universe. It is like a real-time digital test where the option you choose now, leads you to the next question which is entirely different from what it would have been if you had chosen a different option at that point in time.

This thought essentially branches out to indefinite possibilities of lives that you could have lived, instead of your current one.

Too much to take in, is it? Well, what can I say?

Welcome to the World of Multi-verse (or should I say Your Multi-verse of Madness)

I know all this sounds too fancy right now, so let's bring our conversation back to reality.

Instead of cribbing on what could have been and how good your life could have turned out to be, both of which are uncertain and out of your control, what we could focus on is;

- How can I understand myself better from this point on?
- How can I determine my Strengths and Limitations?
- What is the Path that I should take, to be able to make better-informed decisions?
- How do I minimise the errors in my judgement?

Short Answer, **Self Awareness. From the LACK of it to being CONSCIOUS about it. That can make all the difference that you need.**

Remember this: You're only as good as how well you know yourself.

You'll need to conquer yourself before setting out on a journey to conquer the World.

Now the question is, are you willing to CONQUER YOURSELF?
Are you READY for a journey from Striving to Thriving?

If yes, then you're in the right place at the right time. Read on.

The Journey of Self Clarity

To '**Conquer Yourself**' is a rather long journey in itself.

Understanding of Self is not a one-time change, it is a process of '**Constant Evolution**'.

I can hear you asking, '**Where are you in your journey of conquering yourself?**

Well now, let's see…

My journey of Self Awareness started over 9 years ago, through a concept called Dermatoglyphics. Some of you might have heard about it, and some of you might not have. **In simple terms, it is the study and analysis of your 'Fingerprint Patterns'.**

Many years ago, during one of the School Expos that happened here in my city, there was a stall or a booth that caught my attention, which said, 'Analysing your Fingerprints can reveal Your Innate Characteristics'.

Now, that statement was enough to spark my curiosity to know more about what this thing was. And I have been hooked on to learning more and more about this concept ever since. The deeper you understand the concept, the more you realise that there is so much more to learn indeed. Well, the subject of Dermatoglyphics has got enough substance to make its case, there's no doubting that.

But over the course of these 9 years, I've seen people use this very concept positively for learning and teaching, I've seen people abuse the same concept, some people tried to make quick money using some fancy models and very few people, like myself, have dedicated our time to delve deeper into the same to understand the concept better and in learning how to apply our understanding of Dermatoglyphics to make ourselves more conscious, more aware of what we do and why we do things. (that's me trying to build my credibility with you right there ;)

Disclaimer though: I am more interested in the research part of Dermatoglyphics and not so much in selling it in the name of fancy models. However, I use Fingerprint Analysis as one of the tools to get better clarity of our Innate Traits and Abilities.

So the higher and deeper Understanding of Yourself, with me, happens through Fingerprint Analysis but is not a compulsion in your journey. Just saying.

Continuing with the story, getting deeper into the research of Dermatoglyphics, helped me theorise the entire concept in a new light. I started writing my own theory and logic behind the science of Dermatoglyphics around the year 2016. It took me a good part of about 3 years to satisfactorily round up the logic, with a very good amount of accuracy for required aspects of our Innate Characteristics. And what these 3 years taught me was profound. **A Revelation of sorts.**

Whatever I did theorise and whatever logic I was writing, had to be implemented on someone, to begin with, so I decided to be my own test subject for my theory. Sounds a little cliched now when I think back, but it worked wonders for me when it mattered.

Hence began my journey inwards, introspection and vertical coaching on myself, without really knowing what it was at the time. I had to strip open myself of all the egos, self-beliefs, esteems and everything over and above that, which was the only way I could see inside of myself with a clear filter to understand where I was heading and what I was doing.

And trust me when I say this, those 3 years of going deeper within, into my mind, taught me so much about myself that I could never understand in the 25 years before that. This phase changed me as a person and helped me grow as a person. It helped me realise that 'Understanding of Self' is not a one-time change.

And this is the point where you repeat the following statement aloud along with me; go for it… **'Understanding of Self is a process of Constant Evolution.'**

So, are you ready to embark on this journey of Self-clarity with me?

If 'YES' then fasten your seat-belts, this is going to be one heck of a journey.

Your Journey of a Lifetime.

SECTION 4

Are You Ready for a Journey of Your Lifetime?

Now, I understand not everyone feels compelled enough, to dedicate their time just to know more about themselves better. Not years for sure. Right?

You'll only feel compelled when you see the necessity and that necessity starts when you have to make decisions on your own, which typically happens at the time of choosing your career or making any other crucial decision in your Life.

And I don't expect everyone to go through the kind of grind that I went through, to see results or transformation, in terms of Self Clarity. Especially when you feel that you'll have to spend time and money, just to know about yourself better and maybe listen to someone else telling you, what you are good at and what you are not good at. Feels a little Demotivating, isn't it?

- What if, we come up with a process where 'Understanding of Self' is not a task but becomes a daily habit? Would you try it?
- What if, those daily habits make all the difference that you need to inculcate your weekly actions?
- What if, you get someone to keep you accountable for your weekly actions, which can give you your desired monthly results?

- What if, while you understand yourself better, you have a chance to understand the process of 'Analysing Fingerprints' yourself and get trained on it?
- What if, you are given an option to not just spend money but also earn while you contribute using your expertise in Fingerprint Analysis? Would all that then be worth it?

Let me tell you what, if you're a person who's willing to;

- Trust the Process
- Work on your weekly milestones
- Achieve your desired monthly results
- Contribute your learnings and expertise
- Help those looking for results and transformations
- Willing to learn and grow together, because you are not alone in facing your nightmares;

Then, you **SHOULD** definitely make an effort to dedicate time to your Personal Development. Understand yourself better and build your life around the way you are designed and not the other way around. And that would be the beginning of you, living your Life consciously, with yourself.

Once you start to realise the magic of Consciously Living your moments, you'll be surprised to see newer things about yourself that you never knew existed.

So, with that newfound confidence in my theory and a better understanding of Self, I set out to help people like you understand yourself better. Help you look at the aspects of your life in a new light, with a lot more meaning and make better-informed decisions in your life. That's one of the primary keys to not regretting your choices later in life.

All through 2019, I did have quite a few assessments and one-on-one sessions with my clients. Most of them were references from my previous clients and a majority of them turned out to be teen students. And that's when I realised, this is the pain point I need to address, because I have gone through a similar problem during my time as a student due to the lack of clarity and direction, and now these kids are facing the same dilemma.

Interestingly, and oddly enough, it is rather surprising that things haven't changed much from my times, despite having a huge number of professionals working in the Career industry. And that number just seems to be growing by the day.

The root cause of this issue though is not the ability or approach of these career professionals. My understanding is that the problem lies in the assessment part, not in the counselling or coaching of Careers.

How do you assess one's natural abilities and match the correct options available to them when you know, their answers to your questions can always be manipulated by them depending on their mental state at that very moment? (ever heard of Psychometric tests?) That's a rather tall order to ask for, with just Psychometrics, you know.

That's where I come into the picture. All those years of work are not just for me to become a better human being in my life, but to contribute to you about the importance of Self Clarity. *'The clearer you are in your head, the clearer your path becomes'.*

Once you know which path to take, you can approach any sensible Career counsellor or coach to help you take action, but if you are not sure about how to decide on the path, then there's a problem. And that's what is been happening for decades and I am pretty sure this will continue for at least a few more years, despite all of our best efforts.

But, moving in the right direction is important, maybe then we'll be able to multiply the effect and one day, maybe one day, have a comprehensive assessment program reachable to students of all ages to make decisions with more certainty, better clarity and direction.

That is the path I am looking to create.

Now the question that I am trying to answer is, 'How do we make this whole process scalable?'

Well, I think I am pretty close to cracking that code and you'll hear from me soon.

The reason I am focussing on you choosing the right Career niche after Self Clarity is that it's important to make the right choices at that pivotal point of your Life. I know the pain of being stuck in the wrong career, feeling 'maybe you are good for nothing'. And I do not wish to see you go through that kind of uncertainty.

We have all the necessary technology and information today to make the right choices but there are very few and far people in between, to guide us on the right path for our 'Journey of Clarity'.

So now is the time to answer the question of this Section.

Are You Ready to take Your Journey of a Lifetime with me?

If your answer is YES, then you should check out the options of how we can work together. Please feel free to visit MY WEBPAGE whenever you feel ready to take on Your Journey of Self Clarity.

The BIG PURPOSE of my work or the community that I intend to serve is to achieve 'The CLARITY of SELF'

Everything else in your life, including decisions about your Career directions, can be built around your 'Understanding of Self'. That is one of the most efficient ways to live your life consciously, at every moment.

On that note, let's explore the concept of Self-clarity and its importance in our lives, shall we?

A Blueprint to Your Self-clarity

There's a saying which goes something like this, "To understand where you want to go and what you want in life, you need to first understand, who you are and where you stand right now."

Clarity of things is one of the most fundamental aspects that we need to possess in life, and the path to anything clarity starts with that of SELF.

Let me give you an analogy; do you use any of the navigation apps on your smartphone while you're driving or travelling to unfamiliar places? Most of us do, don't we?

I mean, I know I do, so would assume you do too.

No-brainer question: Which is the most popular navigation app in the world? No prizes for guessing here. (I think it's Google Maps, isn't it?)

Just think about this, if you switch off the GPS on your phone and enter the destination that you need to reach, what do you think would happen?

The app won't even start to navigate you around. Do you know why?

That's because even a navigation app needs to know your precise current location to draw out the possible paths to your desired destination.

In simple words, it needs CLARITY on where you are and where you need to go, to show how you can get there. And this repeats for every journey you take, not just a one-time process.

If being aware of your current location is that important to a navigation app to take you through a journey for minutes or maybe a few hours, how is it not important for you to be aware of your current location in this constant journey called LIFE?

Just give it a moment of thought.

Being aware of yourself at every step of life is what it is to live consciously. And for that to happen, your mind's GPS needs to be ON, preferably all the time.

If you follow Sadhguru's talks, you would know, that one of the things he emphasises most, is to live consciously every day, every moment to get the best out of life.

Self-awareness is the word that people commonly associate with all that I've been saying so far, but the problem today is that if you search for the definition of self-awareness online, you get 100s, if not 1000s of different definitions which sound very similar. Hence my attempt to break down the meaning of self-awareness and give you a bit more clarity about yourself.

Well, it might not be entirely different from everything available today, but I am trying to simplify the jargon called self-awareness to its fundamental aspects, that actually matter to us in our everyday life and how this clarity can make a difference in the way we look at things or situations.

Perceptions matter, you see!

As a part of that effort, let's explore those aspects that we would need clarity on, to be more conscious, understand ourselves better and look at life in a new light. Here's a list of things to come:

1. Your Process of Decision-making - An attribution to your PERSONALITY TRAITS
2. Your Identity Matrix - An attribution to your SELF-AWARENESS
3. Your Preferred Learning Environment - An attribution to your SELF-REGULATION
4. Your preferred Career Niche/Working Environment - is based on the attributes of your Identity and Learning environments.
5. Your Energy Matrix - An attribution to your SELF-MOTIVATION
6. Your Communication Preference - An attribution to your EMPATHY

These 6 aspects of Self-clarity are what we are going to explore in the 6 chapters coming up in Part 2 of this book.

Well, with that said, the prep time is up.

Ready to get 'Introduced to Yourself' now?

Parts 2 & 3 of the book are combined together so that it would be easier for you to go through a chapter and a subsequent activity that comes with it.

I sense that you are ready to take on the challenge, so with no further ado, let's get started on your journey of **'Introducing You, to Yourself'**.

Part 2

ASPECTS OF LIFE THAT ACTUALLY MATTER

These 6 Chapters are all you need to get a Better Understanding of Yourself

Here's what you'll find in this Part of the Book

Chapter 1: Your Process of Decision-making - An attribution to your PERSONALITY TRAITS

Activity Section 1: The Wheel of Life

Chapter 2: Your Identity Matrix - An attribution to your SELF-AWARENESS

Activity Section 2: Setting Your S.M.A.R.T. Goals

Chapter 3: Your Preferred Learning Environment - An attribution to your SELF-REGULATION

Activity Section 3: Emotional Intelligence Competency Assessment

Chapter 4: Your preferred Career Niche/Working Environment - is based on the attributes of your Identity and Learning environments.

Activity Section 4: Action Plans

Chapter 5: Your Energy Matrix - An attribution to your SELF-MOTIVATION

Activity Section 5: The Year in Your Life

Chapter 6: Your Communication Preference - An attribution to your EMPATHY

Activity Section 6: Planning & Journaling Your Day

Your Process of Decision-Making

AN ATTRIBUTION TO YOUR PERSONALITY TRAITS

"Everyone makes the best choice available to them, at the time they make it."

– A Presupposition in NLP

Before we talk about the presupposition, let me give you a quick insight into what NLP is about, for those who are not familiar with the term.

The expansion of NLP is Neuro Linguistic Programming.

It is a concept that believes personal change is possible just by a systematic change of thought. It works wonders for those who follow it diligently. Anyway, what is a presupposition in NLP?

A Presupposition is like one of those foundational stones, upon which the concept of NLP, is built.

Now, the one in question here is that which speaks about decision-making. It says, "Everyone makes the best choice available to them, at the time they make it."

The statement itself sounds pretty straight-forward, but what we need to understand are the factors that influence our process of decision-making in that given time.

Why, you ask?

Well, what we decide in any given situation depends on what factor we prioritise the most over the others, along with our awareness of that situation. Let's take a deeper look into what those factors are, and their resultant traits that can eventually define our 'Personality'.

The process of our decision-making can be influenced broadly by 4 factors:

1. **Results** - Prioritises Decision making based on the potential RESULTS of that decision.
2. **Performances** - Prioritises Decision making based on the potential EXPERIENCES that one might get out of that decision.
3. **People** - Prioritises Decision making based on how that decision might affect the PEOPLE and relationships associated with them.
4. **Processes** - Prioritises Decision making based on the DETAILS IN THE PROCESS of that decision.

And each of these factors plays a part in determining our natural PERSONALITY TRAITS that we tend to portray in different situations. And these Personality Traits are defined as shown in the image below.

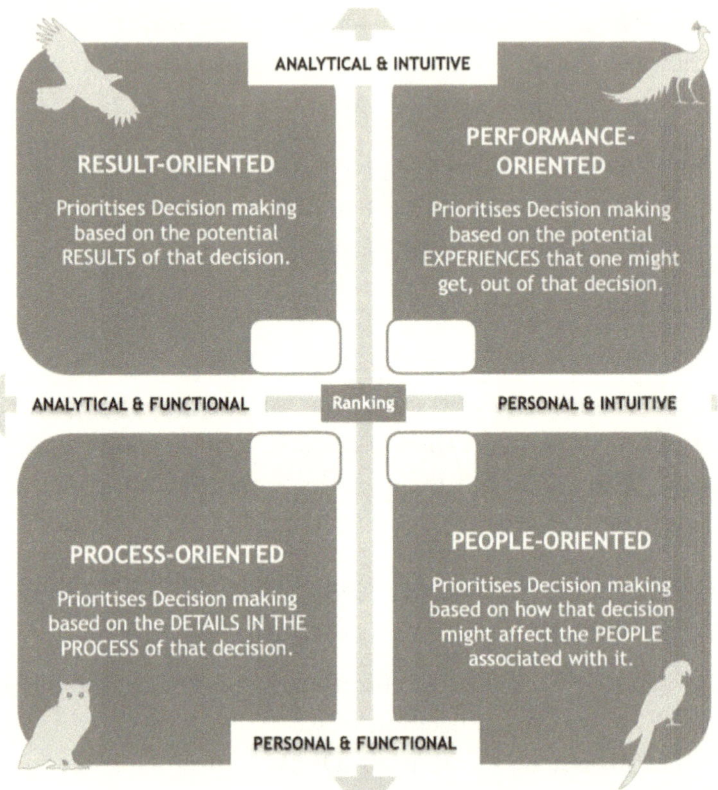

Image 1:   Factors of Decision Making

- **A DOMINATING Personality trait,** primarily influenced by the Result-oriented factor of decision-making, represented by a 'High-flying Eagle'
- **An INSPIRING Personality trait,** primarily influenced by the Performance-oriented factor of decision-making, represented by a 'Beautiful Peacock'
- **An UNDERSTANDING Personality trait,** primarily influenced by the People-oriented factor of decision-making, represented by a 'Happy Parrot'

- **A WISE Personality trait,** primarily influenced by the Process-oriented factor of decision-making, represented by a 'Wise Owl'

Are you starting to resonate with your process of decision-making yet?

Read on, to understand the importance of each of these quadrants better.

Now if you observe all 4 quadrants, the top-left quadrant and the bottom-right quadrant, which are diagonally opposite to each other, are those of Results and People.

Any idea what this means or why they are placed that way?

Well, it means that those who have a stronger inclination toward the result-oriented quadrant, don't really bother to understand what's happening with people around them. If they have to go for results, they will go for it, no matter what the situation is.

On the other hand, those who are naturally more inclined toward the people-oriented quadrant find it difficult to go against the people they are associated, even if it means that they might have to compromise on their goals or results.

Can you relate already?

Let me give you an example to get a better picture of what I am talking about.

Have you watched this movie called Bahubali: The Beginning, the first part of the two movies? In case you haven't, where have you been hiding?

You can go watch this last climax fight seen after reading the book, so that you can connect to this example better, ok?

STORY TIME:

Now, in that movie, there is this sequence during the climax fight scene between the *'Kalakeya Army'* and our Protagonists, i.e., our Heroes.

During this sequence, there's a scene where both Bahubali and Bhallaladeva (those are our Heroes if you are not familiar with the movie) are faced with the same situation even though they fight from different directions.

Just before breaching the inner defences of their enemies and reaching the Kalakeya Lord, the Kalakeya army plays a master stroke.

Out of nowhere, they pull out the people of Mahishmati to form an additional line of defence, making it difficult for our heroes to breach.

Now the situation turned difficult not because these people would fight against our heroes, but because our heroes now had to make a choice. Whether to save their people or get to the Kalakeya Lord?

If you have watched the movie, you know what comes next, who prioritises results, who prioritises people and what happens later in the movie.

The point that I am trying to make here is, though the situation was the same for both Bahubali and Bhallaladeva, who prioritised what, literally defined their character journey in the movie. That defined their PERSONALITY TRAITS.

One goes for a result-at-any-cost approach and the other prioritises people even if that could cost him his result.

So, the few, who are successful in understanding their strengths and being aware of their limitations are those who have learnt to strike a balance between both quadrants in a given situation, taking action accordingly.

Concerning these two quadrants, in particular, something that you need to be wary about is, 'not to lose sight of people around you when you focus on results' and also 'not to lose sight of your results when you're concerned about the people around you'.

The same holds good for the opposite quadrants of Performances and Processes as well.

Those who are strongly inclined towards the process-oriented quadrant tend to make their decisions based on the stability of an idea or a system. Just follow the tried and tested methods of yore to make sure that their decisions don't fail. It's a low risk - low reward quadrant but with consistent and predictable yield. Like our Rahul Dravid's batting, consistent, predictable, stable. No wonder he's called 'The Wall of Indian Cricket'.

On the other hand, those who are more naturally inclined towards the performance-oriented quadrant are those, who prefer taking risks, going with intuition, and living in the moment. More like Virender Sehwag, you ask him to follow the process and take things slow, he'll say "OK" and go smash the next ball.

Well, that's how the decision-making quadrants work, you see..!

So, which one of these quadrants can you resonate with the most?

Remember that, not one quadrant is greater than another in all the given situations and not one quadrant can operate on its own, it will always be influenced by the other quadrants at varying extents, depending on the way you are designed innately.

So, like wolves, your characteristic qualities also tend to hunt you in packs ;)

To sum it up, you tend to make decisions depending on your magnitude of inclination towards these quadrants.

Caution by the wind: If you are a person who tends to have a natural inclination towards opposite quadrants like 'Results & People' or 'Performance & Process', well, best of luck. You'll have a hard time making every decision in life owing to the conflicting natures of those opposite quadrants. Grab on to all the luck you can get.

Well, Jokes apart.

Seriously though, all that matters is, whether YOU take charge of making your decisions or you let YOUR DECISIONS take charge of your life.

Think about it, and you be the best judge of your choices.

The Section Coming Up...

On that note, I would like to introduce the first activity to you in the next section called, 'The Wheel of Life'. It is one of those simple self-assessment tools which can help you be more aware of where you stand currently in different areas of your life. It can be a great levelling tool to ground yourself on how happy or satisfied you are with your life right now, IF YOU'RE HONEST with your rankings, and it can give you a great insight into the areas with maximum room for improvement that you could work on to be happier.

You'll find all the necessary instructions and the document needed to go through the activity in the next section. So see you there and have a great time with YOURSELF.

Let's get started..!

ACTIVITY SECTION 1:
THE WHEEL OF LIFE

Welcome to the first 'Self Assessment' tool in your 'Journey of Self Clarity, called the 'Wheel of Life'.

This tool is nothing new, many coaches, counsellors and psychologists across the globe, use it in their own adapted ways to try and understand the current state of mind of their clients.

And here, we'll be using an adapted version of the Wheel of Life for self-assessment.

All you need to do is rank your ability on each of the parameters given, from 1 to 10 on the sheet given so that it is easier for you to understand which parameters of your life are ranked high and which of them are ranked low, according to you.

(1 being the score of least satisfaction and 10 being the highest)

Here are the parameters and the questions you would need to ask yourself to rank them for your innate satisfaction.

- **Personal Growth** - Are You Consciously Learning Something New Everyday?

  (If you're learning something new every day, then based on your satisfaction with personal growth, you may rank higher, towards the number 10. If you feel lethargic and that you're wasting your time, you may want to rank towards the lower numbers)

- **Career** - Are You in the Right Career or on a Constant Look-out for something else?

  (If you feel you're in the right career and looking to grow with no regrets, then you may look at ranking any number towards the top if not, rank your satisfaction with your career appropriately)

- **Finances** - How Satisfied are You with Your Cash in-flow and out-flow?

  (If you're happy and satisfied with your financial management, you may want to rank higher, if there's room for improvement, then you may rank it accordingly)

- **Health** - Are You Keeping a Tab on Your Physical & Mental Health?

  (If you're conscious about your mental and physical health and you pro-actively take care of yourself, then you may consider ranking yourself a higher number)

- **Family & Friends** - Are You Happy with Your Interactions with Your Immediate Family & Social Circles?

  (If you're happy with people around you and your social interactions with them, then the ranking can be higher, the happier you are, the better would be the ranking)

- **Fun & Recreation** - How often do You take Time-out to Rejuvenate Yourself?

  (If you take time out for personal recreation and spend some quality 'ME TIME', which you enjoy and feel good about, you can rank higher, depending on your sense of satisfaction)

- **Relationships** - How Comfortable are You with the person in Your Intimate Relationship?

(Ranking of this part, as everything else, of your Wheel of Life, corresponds to how happy you're in the relationship with your spouse/girlfriend/boyfriend, the happier you're, the higher would be the ranking)

If you're being too honest in answering this, then you might want to consider hiding it from your spouse/girlfriend/boyfriend, don't tell me that I didn't warn you. #justsaying ;)

- **Physical Environment** - How Pleasant or Comfortable is Your Physical Environment around You?

(If you feel happy and satisfied when you look around where you're right now, as you work on your assessment, your ranking may be considered higher, if you feel you feel suffocated by your physical surroundings and need to be better, you may consider a lower ranking accordingly)

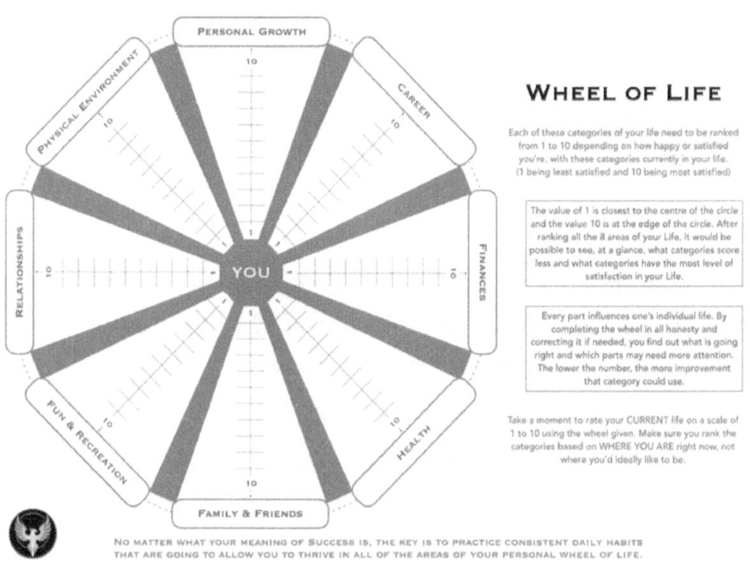

Image 2:   Wheel of Life

So this is your Wheel of Life. Once you have marked all the rankings on the sheet, you can connect each of your rankings to form a nice spider graph, which gives you a clear indication of those areas of your life where you have the most satisfaction and those areas with the most room for improvement.

Based on your results, you might need to work on the areas which are ranked low.

Pro Tip: You know why you scored some parameters low, so you know what you need, to get a higher rank in those areas, all that's left to do is take appropriate action to make things better.

The key to using this tool effectively is YOUR HONESTY. You are not doing this assessment to impress anybody, please do keep this in mind. You're doing this to understand the current realities of your life.

Rankings should be based on your current reality in each of the parameters. Not your past, not your future, just the PRESENT.

Hope this honest assessment helps you stay with yourself and lets you think about yourself for a considerable amount of time, to make necessary changes so that you can lead a happier and more satisfying life.

Like most things in our lives, this assessment is not a one-time thing. You can revisit and re-rank Your Wheel of Life as frequently as you deem necessary, preferably once every 3 months so that you become more aware of the changes happening in your life.

That's all for now, have a great time with yourself in figuring out Your Wheel of Life and I'll see you on the other side.

CHAPTER 2

Your Identity Matrix

AN ATTRIBUTION TO YOUR SELF-AWARENESS

"It's always better to conquer yourself before you set out on a journey to conquer the World."

– An Ancient Saying

The Identity Matrix is about answering one question.

How would you want to be identified or remembered after your time?

It is about understanding what your natural traits tend to prioritise when it comes to identifying & associating yourself with the outer world.

You may need to recognise and understand your own moods, motivations and their effect on others. To achieve this state, you must be able to monitor your own emotional state and identify your emotional triggers.

Attribute: SELF AWARENESS

Self-awareness is the ability to accurately recognise your emotions, strengths, limitations, and actions to understand how these affect your 'BEING' and that of those around you.

Once you have a better understanding of self-awareness, you tend to grow into a better version of yourself by identifying your strengths, understanding your limitations and planning your life accordingly. But for that to happen, you need to be clear about the type of identity that you can associate with, the most.

Your identity traits are formed by how you think and what you do, irrespective of what situations you're surrounded by. In other words, the processing of your thoughts and reasoning for your actions that you deem best fit in a given situation inherently forms your identity. And combinations of those identities are what form Your Identity Matrix.

Remember the factors that we saw earlier, which would affect your decision-making process?

While these 4 factors of influence, namely;

- **Results**
- **Performances**
- **People**
- **Processes**

are going to remain constant through all the other chapters that you go through, it is the combinations of these factors that would form respective quadrants in each chapter.

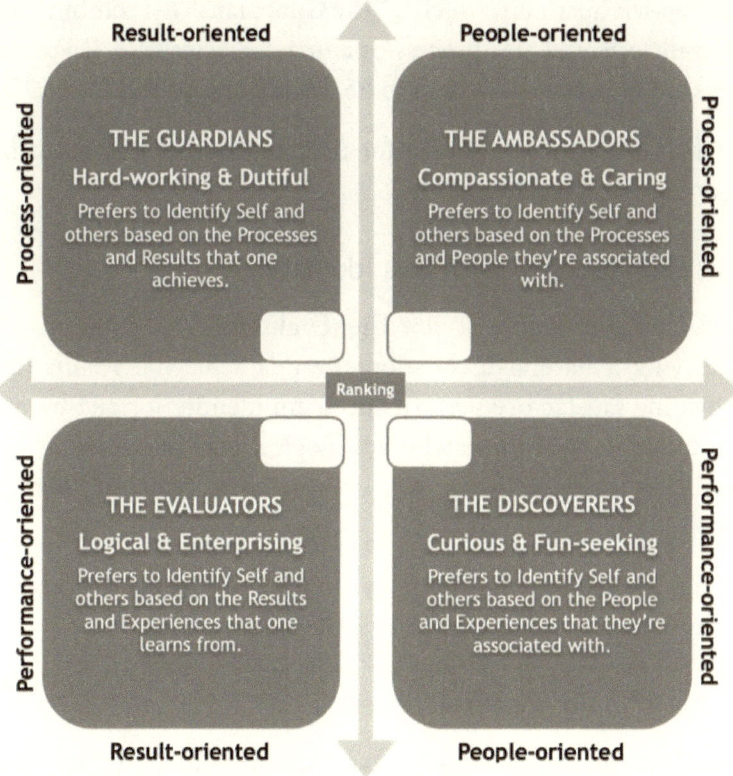

Image 3:   Identity Matrix

Similar to the quadrants that we saw in the previous chapter, here are the 4 quadrants of your identity matrix.

1. **The Guardians** - who are 'Hardworking & Dutiful'
2. **The Evaluators** - who are 'Logical & Enterprising'
3. **The Ambassadors** - who are 'Caring & Compassionate'
4. **The Discoverers** - who are 'Curious & Fun-seeking'

Referring to the image of the identity matrix quadrants;

The top-left quadrant, which is **'The Guardians'**, is a combination of result-oriented and process-oriented characteristics. These are the kind of people who tend to be 'Hardworking and Dutiful'.

- The Guardians are known for their practicality and focus on order, security and stability.

Can you resonate with this identity?

The quadrant below it is **'The Evaluators'**, a combination of having a natural inclination towards achieving results and delivering satisfactory performances. An identity formed by this combination is of those who are 'Logical and Enterprising', an ideal combination for you to have that entrepreneurial drive in you.

- The Evaluators are typically known for their rationality, impartiality and intellectual excellence.

Is this who you naturally are?

The third quadrant, which is at the top-right, is called **'The Ambassadors›** which is formed by a combination of people and process-oriented characteristics in you. The qualities of this identity are portrayed in being 'Caring and Compassionate'.

- The Ambassadors are known for their empathy, diplomatic skills and passionate idealism. They might have some strong opinions but they tend to deal with a lot of care and responsibility.

Are any bells ringing yet?

The final quadrant of the identity matrix is that of **'The Discoverers›**. This quadrant is formed by the combination of people-oriented and performance-oriented characteristics. These are the kind of people who tend to be 'Curious and Fun-seeking', those who believe that journeys in life are more important than the destination itself. Explore new worlds, and experience new things.

- The Discoverers are known for their spontaneity, ingenuity and flexibility.

Are you one of those to whom experiences matter more than results?

Which of these quadrants or combinations do you think are natural to you?

Again as mentioned during your decision-making journey, there is no right or wrong identity trait. Each of us is unique and different by design at some level, so we naturally tend to enjoy different experiences, and thrive in different situations.

It is upon us to understand our identity traits, embrace them and pursue our goals based on our strengths and not get stuck in a rat race, playing to someone else's strengths.

Enough food for thought?

Now that we have an idea of where your strengths and limitations might be, it is time to figure out how to put them to use.

The Section Coming Up...

On that note, I would like to introduce you to an activity to set your goals. It is called "Setting Your S.M.A.R.T. Goals". You can set your goals depending on your dominant quadrant and the factors that matter to you the most.

Now, what are S.M.A.R.T. Goals and how to set them is what you'll find in the next section. Go ahead and get it done.

See you on the other side.

Let's go..!

ACTIVITY SECTION 2: SETTING YOUR S.M.A.R.T. GOALS

What are **S.M.A.R.T.** goals, why is it important and what are the questions that you'll need to answer for yourself, to get a better understanding of which way you want to head towards in life?

Let's get started, shall we?

The abbreviation of **S.M.A.R.T.** is about defining goals that are;

- **SPECIFIC**
- **MEASURABLE**
- **ACHIEVABLE**
- **RELEVANT &**
- **TIME-BOUND**

The **S.M.A.R.T.** model of goal setting is one of the most popular models out there because it is fairly simple yet amazingly effective.

Below are the questions you need to answer to stay on track with your goal-setting process.

Image 4: S.M.A.R.T. Goals

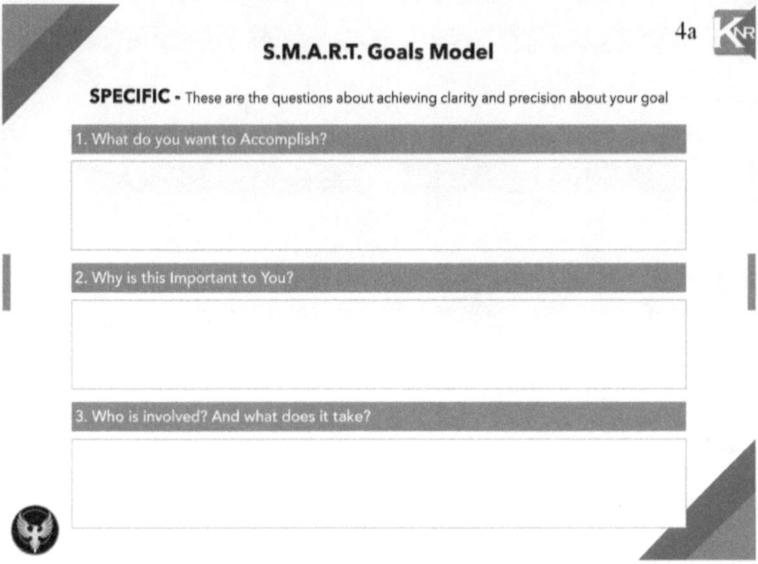

4a

S.M.A.R.T. Goals Model

SPECIFIC - These are the questions about achieving clarity and precision about your goal

1. What do you want to Accomplish?

2. Why is this Important to You?

3. Who is involved? And what does it take?

1. **SPECIFIC** - These are the questions about achieving clarity and precision in your goal

- What do you want to Accomplish?
- Why is this Important to You?
- Who is involved? And what does it take?

Additional Notes:

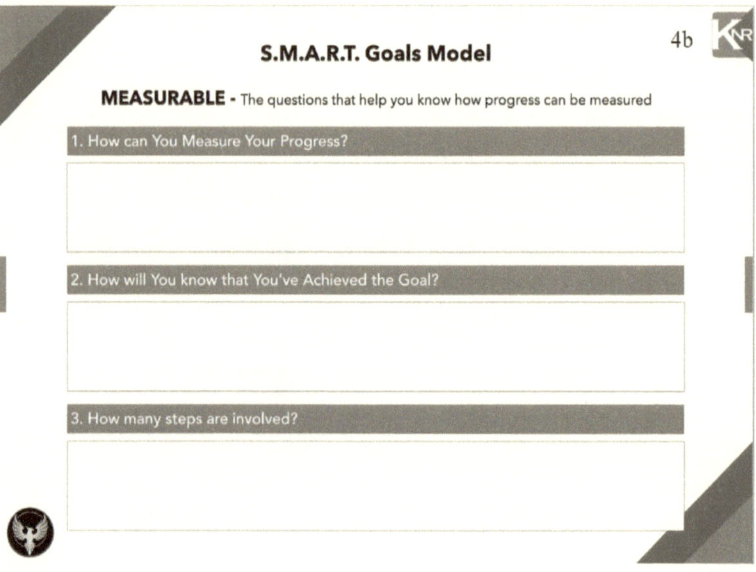

2. MEASURABLE - The questions that help you know how to understand your progress

- How Can You Measure Your Progress?
- How will You know that You've Achieved the Goal?
- How many steps are involved?

Additional Notes:

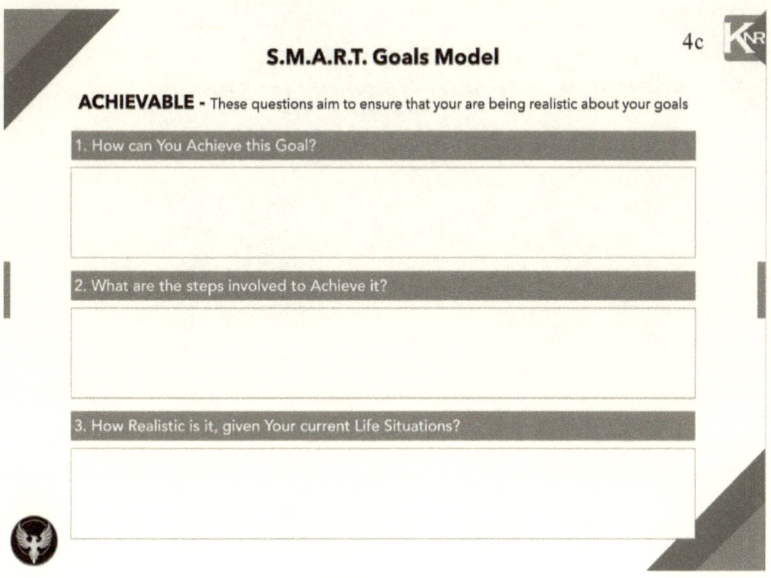

3. ACHIEVABLE - These questions aim to ensure that you are being realistic about your goals

- How Can You Achieve this Goal?
- What are the steps involved to Achieve it?
- How Realistic is it, given Your current Life Situations?

Additional Notes:

S.M.A.R.T. Goals Model

4d

RELEVANT - These questions help you stay committed to the goal and not lose motivation along the way

1. Does the Goal seem Worthwhile?

2. Is this the Right Time to Act?

3. Do You have Adequate Resources to Achieve the Goal?

4. RELEVANT - These questions help you stay committed to the goal and not lose motivation along the way

- Does the Goal seem Worthwhile at this point?
- Is this the Right Time to Act?
- Do You Have Adequate Resources to Achieve the Goal?

Additional Notes:

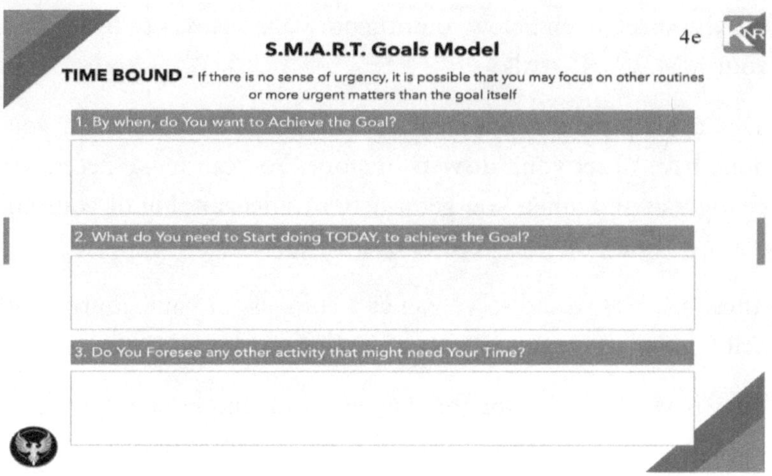

5. TIME-BOUND - If there is no sense of urgency, you may focus on other routines or more urgent matters than the goal itself

- When do You want to Achieve the Goal?
- What do You need to start doing TODAY, to achieve the Goal?
- Do You Foresee any other activity that might need Your Time?

Additional Notes:

The questions are pretty straight forward and answering these 15 questions with honesty, will give you enough time for yourself and understand the way you look at your goals. Please refer to the activity sheet given below to bring out your answers to figure out your S.M.A.R.T. goals.

This is a simple yet powerful activity and the best part is you don't have to set your answers in stone. You can make necessary changes as and when you get a better understanding of yourself and the situations you need to deal with.

These answers would serve you as a compass in your 'Journey of Self Clarity'.

That is your activity for the day, you can simply take a look at the S.M.A.R.T. Goals template document provided below, write down your answers and keep them as a reference to not lose track of why you started this journey in the first place.

Hope you have a great time and remember this document is your compass on this long winding journey.

Again HONESTY is the key, have fun.

CHAPTER 3

Your Preferred Learning Environment

AN ATTRIBUTION TO YOUR SELF-REGULATION

"Tell me and I forget. Teach me and I remember. Involve me and I LEARN."

– Benjamin Franklin

How involved do you think you can be with your Learning Environment?

My coach often says, "Your Environment is Stronger than Your Will Power."

Very true, isn't it? No matter how badly you want to do something, if your immediate environment doesn't support you, you wouldn't be able to succeed.

Well, let me give you an example.

What do you think would happen if you are taken to Mars and are asked to get used to that environment? How long do you think it would take before you give up in an environment, that's not suited for you?

Before you answer that, let's look at what Self Regulation has to do with your Environment, shall we?

Being in the right environment is essential in controlling your impulses—instead of being quick to react rashly, you can reign in your emotions and think before responding, thereby reducing unnecessary tensions and behaving appropriately, often referred to as maturity.

Attribute: SELF REGULATION

Self-regulation allows you to, wisely manage your emotions and impulses - you show or restrain certain emotions depending on what is necessary and beneficial for the situation. And understanding what kind of environment helps you thrive and

what kind can suffocate you, helps you regulate your emotions in the best way possible.

Now going back to Mars, when you know you're designed to breathe and live here on Earth, isn't it wise to stay in an environment, that doesn't suffocate you?

Once the environment you live in goes out of hand, that's when your intrinsic ability to regulate your emotions becomes negligible, resulting in unnecessary actions and thoughts.

Well, you may ask me, "Doesn't staying in a safer environment, get you used to being in your COMFORT-ZONE?"

All that I am saying is, that if you want to try out a challenging environment to learn something new or achieve something great, go ahead and do it. Just don't get stuck there if it starts to get toxic. You would have heard of, or experienced choosing the wrong course, the wrong career, or being in the wrong relationship (personal or professional), all of these have higher tendencies of turning toxic if your preferences are not taken care of.

So be it 'in the family' or 'to learn' or 'at work', you need to identify the right living environment for you, to thrive and not feel drained.

Just because you're feeling adventurous and want to visit Mars, doesn't mean the environment there will be favourable for you to breathe. You'll need a lot more extra resources, both internal and external, for you to even survive on Mars, let alone thrive and create a favourable habitat.

So here's my suggestion, 'Don't stay stuck on Mars when you know your resources don't suit its environment. Find your Earth and breathe easy, breathe happily.'

Oh, by the way, if you're really feeling too adventurous about wanting to try out the Martian Environment, then you should probably talk to Elon Musk. Not a bad idea that, right?

Anyway, how do you identify the right environment, you ask?

Well, to identify the right environment for you, you'll need to understand the influence of the same 4 factors that we have been talking about in the last two chapters, on your environment. So here it goes:

1. **Results:** if you prefer to be with people talking and focussing on data and results all the time
2. **Performances:** if you prefer being with people who can motivate you with their energy and positive vibes to bring out the best in you
3. **People:** if you prefer being with people who can lend you emotional support when you feel low or down
4. **Processes:** if you prefer being with people who value your consistency and stability in the way you do things

The combinations of these 4 factors would determine your preferred 'Learning Styles' which would essentially lead to understanding the kind of ENVIRONMENT that you need to create around yourself to nurture your LEARNING STYLES.

Let's take a look at the kind of Learning Styles that are broadly accepted, shall we?

According to the VARK model, learners are identified by their preferences for 4 types of learning:

- **Visual learning** (pictures, movies, diagrams)

  Visual learners learn best by seeing or observing things visually. Graphic displays such as charts, diagrams, illustrations, handouts, and videos are all helpful learning tools for visual learners.

- **Auditory learning** (music or rhymes, discussions, audio content)

  Aural (or auditory) learners learn best by hearing or listening to information. They tend to get a great deal out of lectures and are good at remembering things they are told about.

- **Reading and writing** (making lists, reading textbooks, taking notes)

  Reading and writing learners prefer to take in and present information that is displayed as words or text. You can see them taking a lot of notes in between discussions.

- **Kinaesthetic learning** (movement, experiments, hands-on activities)

  Kinaesthetic (or tactile) learners learn best through experiences, practical, hands-on learning. The more familiar they get with the sense of touch or tactile, the more comfortable they are to learn.

Again, as with every other aspect of the way you're designed, these learning preferences also always work in combinations, they cannot work individually, hence we'll need to consider the combined preferences for your environments to learn, grow, work or live.

There are 4 different types of Learning Environments that we can consider:

1. **Goal-oriented Environment** - which is essential to nurture your visual learning preference, tends to thrive in achieving results with a preference for Visual aids. This is an environment which is preferred by people who want to be the best in what they do and love to be recognised for achieving their results.
2. **Enthusiastic Environment** - which is essential to nurture your kinaesthetic learning preference, tends to thrive in a competitive and motivating environment with a preference for Experiential Learning. This is a kind of environment that is suited more for sporting or athletic individuals.
3. **Group-based Environment** - which is essential to nurture your auditory learning preference, tends to thrive in a team environment with a preference for Auditory Learning. The kind-of environment for people who are better at remembering or understanding concepts while discussing in groups, bouncing off their ideas or when they're teaching to others.
4. **Individualistic Environment** - which is essential to nurture your Read-write learning preference, tends to thrive in a step-by-step learning environment with a preference towards engaging in Text Content. An environment, that is typically preferred by people who like to lock themselves up and learn or execute things on their own without getting disturbed.

Now that you have an idea about the different kinds of Learning Environments, which one of these do you think would suit you the most?

Can you rank them from 1 to 4 on the image given below? (1 being the most suitable and 4 being the least suitable for you)

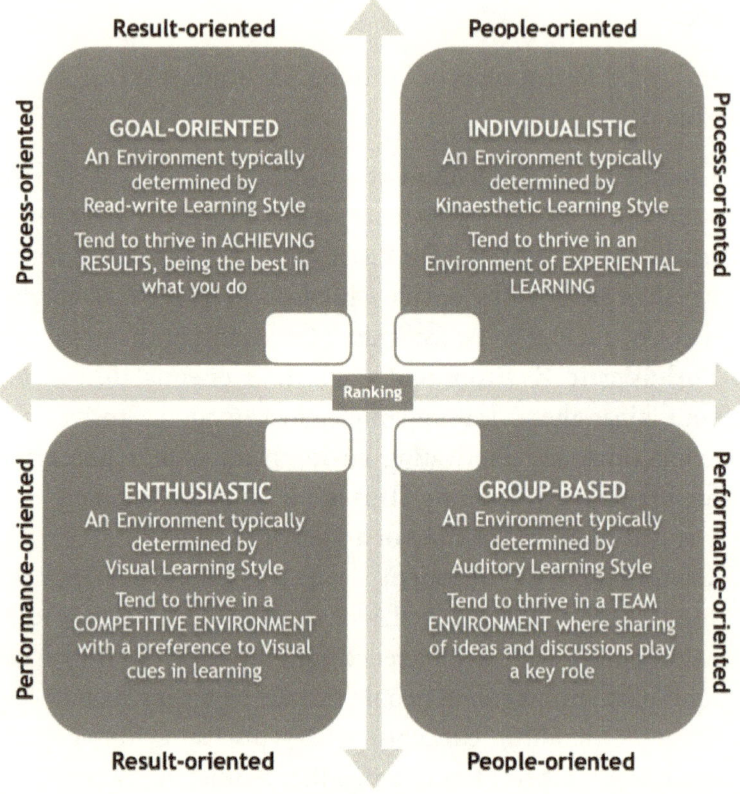

Image 5: Learning Environments

I do know that understanding learning environments is not as straightforward as the parameters of decision-making or the personalities of the identity matrix. It has another layer of understanding your learning preferences (or learning styles) that is necessary.

However, if you go by the similarities of each chapter that we discuss in this book, you'll see that they are not too different from one another, at least in terms of how the concepts are laid out for you to understand.

All the quadrants that you see in every chapter are combinations of the 4 influencing factors called;

RESULTS, PERFORMANCES, PEOPLE & PROCESSES.

So feel free to refer back to the previous chapters if you need a sense of familiarity between the combinations of different quadrants.

Understanding your preference for Learning Environments is crucial because, the selection of Career Niches, which we'll deal with in the next chapter, depends on your natural preference for learning environments and your identity matrix at large.

Random Gyaan: Interested in some random gyaan (information for its sake)??

Ready or not, here it comes...

Skills can be learnt, and mindsets can be changed but the core design of your mind doesn't really change. If you are wrong about doing something, you'll inherently feel wrong about doing it, no matter how long you think about it. And that's exactly why this particular aspect of life, SELF REGULATION, is compared to your 'Mental Brick Wall'. Not the ones that your society feeds you, Societally constructed walls can be demolished if the integrity that defines you is strong enough but the ones that you inherently feel, they're almost impossible to break. The superficial beliefs that you build for yourself, they're difficult to deal with if you can't come to terms with what your life has to offer you.

Trying to be more conscious about what you do and BEING IN THE PRESENT is what matters in most situations.

There are lots of people doing things that they don't resonate with even today. Make no mistake, but at the end of the day, those who know how to define satisfaction in life, know the value of staying righteous to their own being and not succumbing to external pressures, in this case, their ENVIRONMENTS.

Enough gyaan already, now back to REALITY...

Now that you're aware of the different types of environments, can you answer our very first question of this chapter;

How involved do you think you are with your Learning Environments?

In a nutshell, it's extremely important to understand and stay in an environment where you can thrive and not get suffocated. The more involved you are in your suitable environment, the better it is for you to learn. Challenging environments are good to learn something new in the short term but never getting stuck in it for the long term. Please be mindful of it and try to get out of there before things turn toxic.

Can you do that for yourself? PLEASE.

The Section Coming Up...

Anyway, that's it for this chapter, you can now head on to the next section for some EI-based Competency Assessment where you'll get to know more about the parameters of Self-awareness, Self-management, Social-awareness and Relationship-management.

Have fun and I'll see you on the other side..!

ACTIVITY SECTION 3: EMOTIONAL INTELLIGENCE COMPETENCY ASSESSMENT

In this activity, we'll be going through a competency assessment, based on your Emotional Intelligence. Again, please BE HONEST with your answers, we are not trying to impress anybody with high scores but trying to understand ourselves better about where we stand at this point.

EI-based 'Competency Assessment' is made up of 4 core skills that pair up under two primary competencies:

1. **Personal Competence**
2. **Social Competence**

It affects how we manage behaviour, navigate social complexities and makes personal decisions to achieve positive results.

Emotional Intelligence is that intangible ability in us that, when focussed on, enhances our levels of self-awareness and the awareness of our surroundings.

Personal Competence is made up of your self-awareness and self-management skills, which focus more on you as an individual rather than on your interactions with other people. It is your ability to stay aware of your emotions and manage your behaviour and tendencies.

CORE SKILLS OF PERSONAL COMPETENCE:

- **Self Awareness** is your ability to accurately perceive your emotions and stay aware of them as they happen.
- **Self Management** is your ability to use your emotional awareness and stay flexible that positively directs your behaviour.

In Personal Competence, 'Self Awareness' is 'What You See' and 'Self Management' is 'What You Do'

Social Competence is made up of social awareness and relationship management skills. In fact, it is your ability to understand other people's moods, behaviours and motives to improve the quality of your relationships.

CORE SKILLS OF SOCIAL COMPETENCE:

- **Social Awareness** is your ability to accurately pick up on emotions in other people and understand what is going on.
- **Relationship Management** is your ability to use awareness of your emotions and that of the others to manage your interactions successfully.

In Social Competence, 'Social Awareness' is 'What You See' and 'Relationship Management' is 'What You Do'

Parameters of EI Competency Assessment:

In this activity, you're provided with 3 parameters in each of the 4 core skills. You'll have to rank your abilities based on your understanding of your core skills from 1 to 10 (1 being the least competent and 10 being the most competent in you)

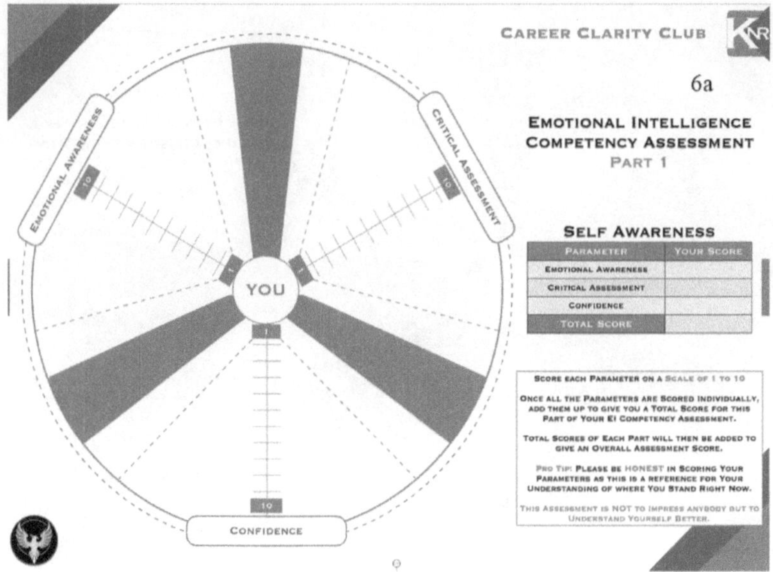

Image Series 6:   EI Competency Assessment

In Self Awareness

- **Emotional Awareness:** Ability to Recognise feelings and how they affect YOU
- **Critical Assessment:** Ability to Recognise strengths, and shortcomings and focus on how to improve
- **Confidence:** Ability to Present Yourself in an assured, impressive, and an unhesitating manner

Additional Notes:

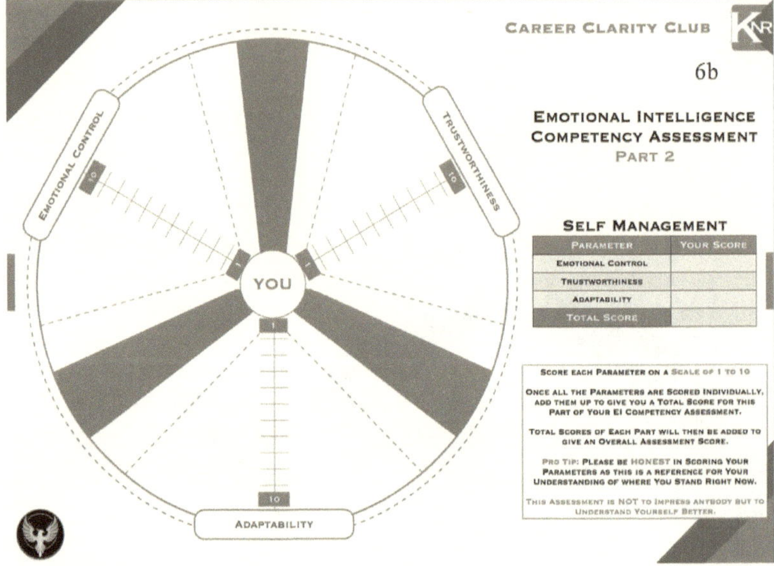

In Self Management

- **Emotional Control:** Ability to Stay calm, unflappable, and clear-headed in high-stress situations
- **Trustworthiness:** Ability to Openly admit faults or mistakes and confront unethical behaviour
- **Adaptability:** Ability to be comfortable with ambiguities and adapt to new challenges

Additional Notes:

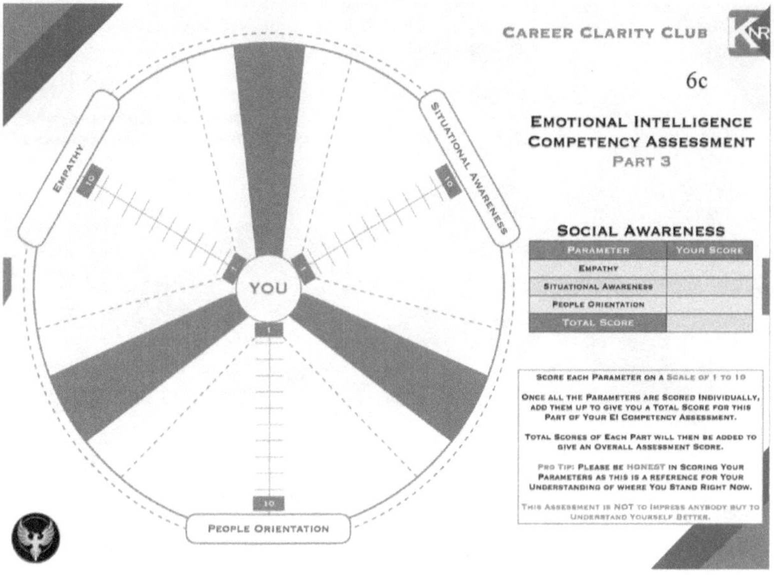

In Social Awareness

- **Empathy:** Ability to understand other's perspectives and stay open to diversity
- **Situational Awareness:** Ability to Understand the vibes and unspoken gravity of the situation
- **People Orientation:** Ability to be proactive about caring for others and addressing underlying concerns

Additional Notes:

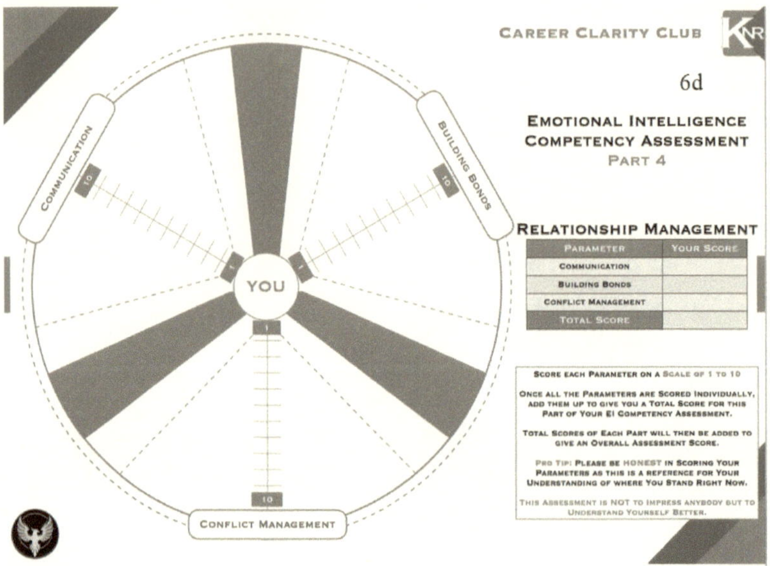

In Relationship Management

- **Communication:** Ability to effectively convey messages and understand the 'How' language of Your Audience
- **Building Bonds:** Ability to Build strong friendships and meaningful relationships with people of all kinds
- **Conflict Management:** Ability to Understand all sides of the conflict and find common ideals to resolve it

Additional Notes:

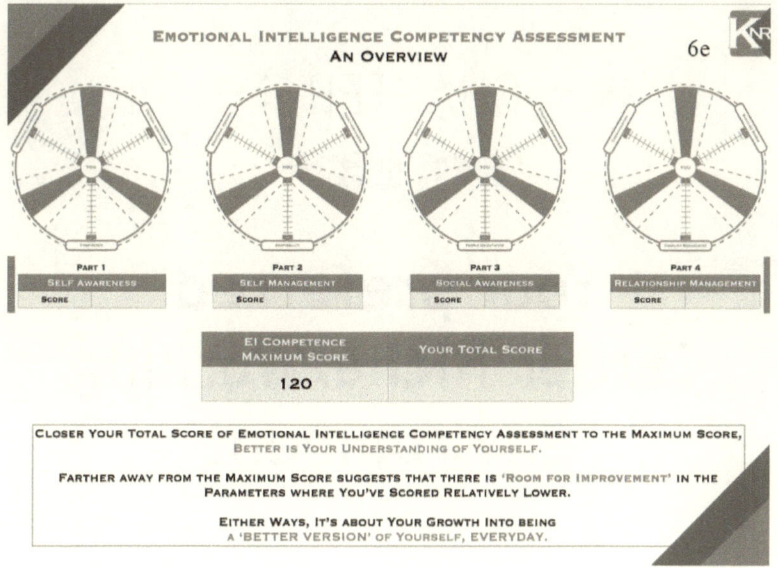

These are the parameters that need to be ranked and all you have to do is go to the 'EI Competency Assessment' document, provided on the next page and rank the parameters based on the understanding of your Emotional Intelligence skills.

Each of these 4 core skills, can be enhanced by being more conscious and aware of 'What You See' and 'What You Do' at every step of your life.

Take your time and please do finish this activity before moving on to the next chapter. There's no hurry, whatsoever.

I'll see you on the other side shortly.

CHAPTER 4

Your preferred Career Niche/Working Environment

"What I know, is that if you do work that you love and the work fulfils you, the rest will come."

– Oprah Winfrey

In the chapters so far, we focussed on gaining Clarity of Self, using some assessments and activities. With a newfound understanding of yourself, let's try to explore where your abilities and preferences match in terms of Career Niches.

These Career Niches are based on John Holland's 'Theory of Careers'. But before we get there, let's do a quick recap of the two most important aspects discussed in the previous chapters, required to talk about choosing your Career Niche:

1. **Understanding Your Identity Matrix**
2. **Your Preferred Learning Environments**

Step 1:

Identity Matrix defines the different combinations of personalities a person can have, which in turn defines his or her 'Identity'. Now Identity matrix can be defined as quadrants, each of them with its own quality.

Here are the names of these quadrants, followed by their characteristic nature, you can download the image of this 'Identity Matrix' using the link provided below this video. So the quadrants are as follows:

The Guardians - who are 'Hardworking & Dutiful'
- The Guardians are known for their practicality and focus on order, security and stability.

The Evaluators - who are 'Logical & Enterprising'
- The Evaluators are known for their rationality, impartiality and intellectual excellence.

The Ambassadors - who are 'Caring & Compassionate'
- The Ambassadors are known for their empathy, diplomatic skills and passionate idealism. They might have some strong opinions but they tend to deal with a lot of care and responsibility.

The Discoverers - who are 'Curious & Fun-seeking'
- The Discoverers are known for their spontaneity, ingenuity and flexibility.

For more details, you can refer back to Chapter 2 - Understanding Your Identity Matrix.

Now that we have an idea about the identity matrix, which of these personalities do you think you are most inclined towards?

Make note of your identity matrix ranking in 'Image 7', you'll need it to figure out your preferred career niche.

Step 2:

The next concept we need to remember is Your Preference for Learning Environments. To identify your preferred learning environments, you need to know the different types of environments that can be considered and they are as follows:

Goal-oriented Environment - which is essential to nurture your visual learning preference, tends to thrive in achieving results with a preference for Visual aids.

Enthusiastic Environment - which is essential to nurture your kinaesthetic learning preference, tends to thrive in a competitive and motivating environment with a preference for Experiential Learning.

Group-based Environment - which is essential to nurture your auditory learning preference, tends to thrive in a team environment with a preference for Auditory Learning.

Individualistic Environment - which is essential to nurture your Read-write learning preference, tends to thrive in a step-by-step learning environment with a preference towards engaging in Text Content.

Again, for more details, you can refer back to Chapter 3 - Your Preferred Learning Environments.

Now that you have an idea about the different kinds of Learning Environments,

which one of these learning environments, do you think would suit you the most?

Make note of the rankings in 'Image 8' for your most preferred environments to learn, work or grow in.

Please refer to the images 7 & 8 for you to make note of the rankings from Your Identity Matrix and Your Learning Environments.

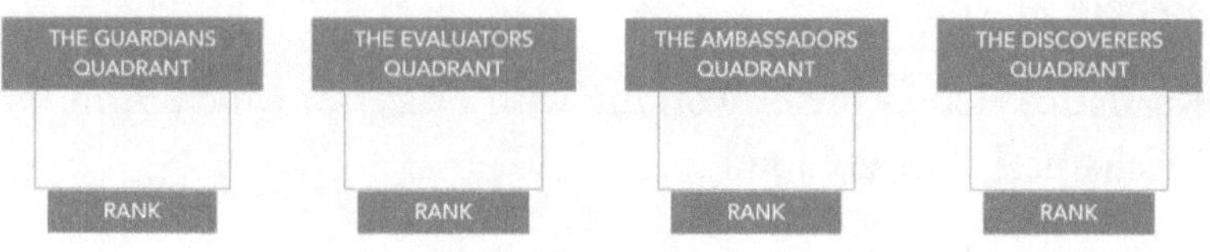

Image 7:   Identity Matrix Ranking

Replicate the 'RANKINGS' of each of these quadrants from your 'Identity Matrix' chapter and your 'Learning Environments' chapter.

Use the combination of these rankings to determine the best suited 'Career Niche' for your Natural Traits.

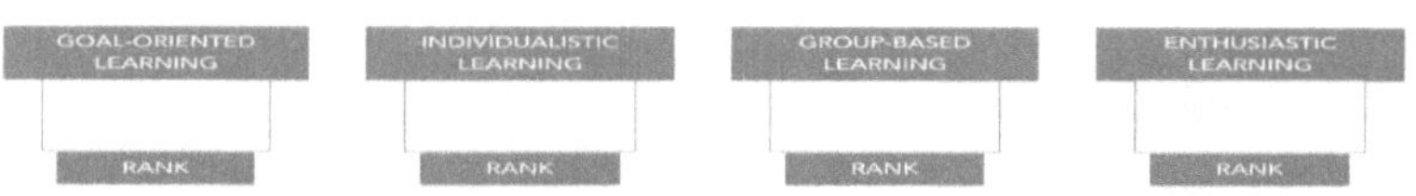

Image 8:   Learning Environments Ranking

Step 3:

Once you make note of the rankings of both 'Your Preferred Identity' and 'Your Preferred Learning Environment', the next step is to identify Career Niches based on your preferences.

Let's take a look at the 6 Career Niches and you can figure out which Career Niche suits you the most, based on the identity and learning environment preferences that you have made note of.

So here we go..!

Realistic Niche - prefer working with Processes which form the Mechanical Career Cloud

- Preferred Identity - Hardworking & Dutiful
- Preferred Learning Environment - Individualistic

Investigative Niche - prefer working with Processes and Ideas which form the Science & Technology Career Cloud

- Preferred Identity - A combination of Hardworking & Dutiful while being Curious & Fun-seeking
- Preferred Learning Environment - A combination of Individualistic and Enthusiastic

Artistic Niche - prefer working with Ideas and People who form the Arts Career Cloud

- Preferred Identity - A combination of Curious & Fun-seeking while being Caring & Compassionate
- Preferred Learning Environment - A combination of Enthusiastic and Group-based

Social Niche - prefer working with People which form the Social Services Career Cloud

- Preferred Identity - Caring & Compassionate
- Preferred Learning Environment - Group-based

Entrepreneurial Niche - prefer working with People & Data which form the Administration & Sales Career Cloud

- Preferred Identity - A combination of Caring & Compassionate while being Logical & Enterprising

- Preferred Learning Environment - A combination of Group-based and Goal-based

Conventional Niche - prefer working with Data & Processes which form the Business Operations Career Cloud

- Preferred Identity - A combination of Logical & Enterprising while being Hardworking & Dutiful
- Preferred Learning Environment - A combination of Goal-based and Individualistic

Now out of all these career niches, Entrepreneurial and Investigative Niches are different. They need you to have preferences for unusual combinations of Identity and Learning Environments. This reflects the reason, why the number of people who excel in these two Niches is way lesser than in the others.

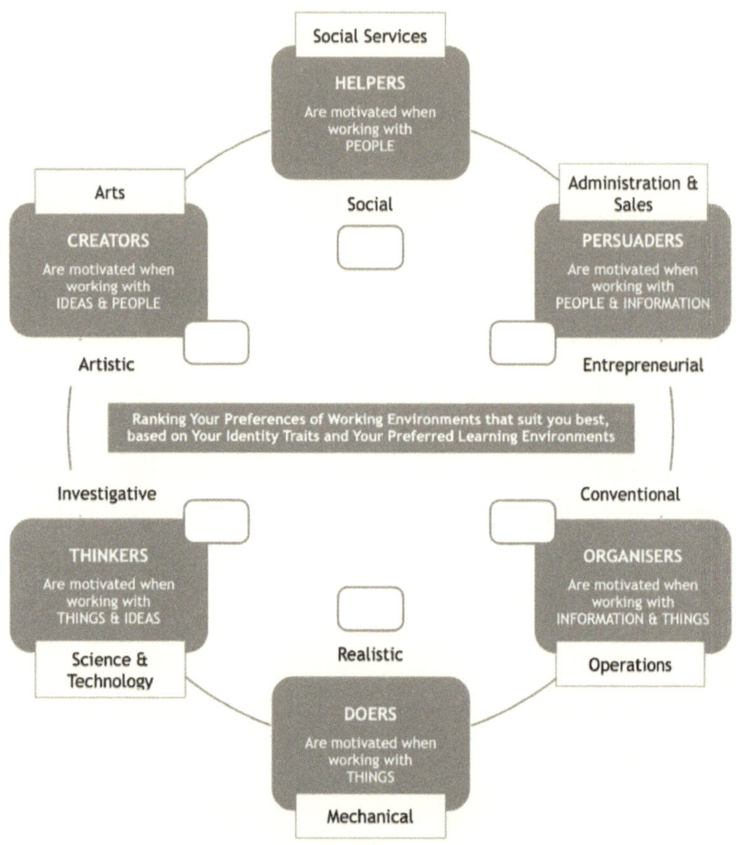

Image 9:   Career Niche Selection

Could you now identify your Career Niche?

If yes, could you rank the Career Niches that you think suit you the most from 1 to 6 (Rank 1 being your most suited niche and 6 being the least suited niche)?

Super, have a great time choosing the Career Niche of Your Preference and I'll see you in the next section.

The Section Coming Up...

Now that you have an idea about your preference in Career Niche, let's try and set an Action Plan for your goals in the next section, shall we?

Every section of every chapter is interrelated. Hence, if you've not completed the task of Setting your S.M.A.R.T. goals yet, then now is the time to do it.

You can either set a short-term goal of 3 months or a long-term goal of 1 year. You can use the Action Plan template depending on the type of goal you set for yourself. So, get going with your goals and action plans. I'll see you on the other side. Have fun.

ACTIVITY SECTION 4: ACTION PLANS

Hope you had a great time with the EI Competency Assessment in your previous activity section.

Now it's time to focus on the goal that you set during your S.M.A.R.T. goals section that you would like to achieve by this time next year and try and break down an 'Action Plan' to achieve it. Are you ready?

Let's get started..!

In case you still haven't worked on your S.M.A.R.T. goals activity, now is the time to do it. Write down that ONE GOAL you would like to achieve in the next ONE year.

Just a RECAP of what S.M.A.R.T. Goals are.

The abbreviation of **S.M.A.R.T.** is about defining goals that are;

- **S**PECIFIC: These are the questions about achieving clarity and precision in your goal
- **M**EASURABLE: The questions that help you know how to understand your progress
- **A**CHIEVABLE: These questions aim to ensure that you are being realistic about your goals
- **R**ELEVANT: These questions help you stay committed to the goal and not lose motivation along the way
- **T**IME-BOUND: If there is no sense of urgency, you may focus on other routines or more urgent matters than the goal itself

The **S.M.A.R.T.** model of goal setting is one of the most popular models out there because it is fairly simple yet amazingly effective.

Once you're ready with the goal, it's time to break down your goal in terms of time.

Firstly, break down your ONE-YEAR goal into two parts that can be achieved in 6 months each. Now each of the 6 months, needs to be further broken down into smaller time durations to define the monthly checkpoints, weekly milestones and daily tasks.

You are given a template on the next page, to break down your action plans for your one-year goal.

Let's look at them one by one.

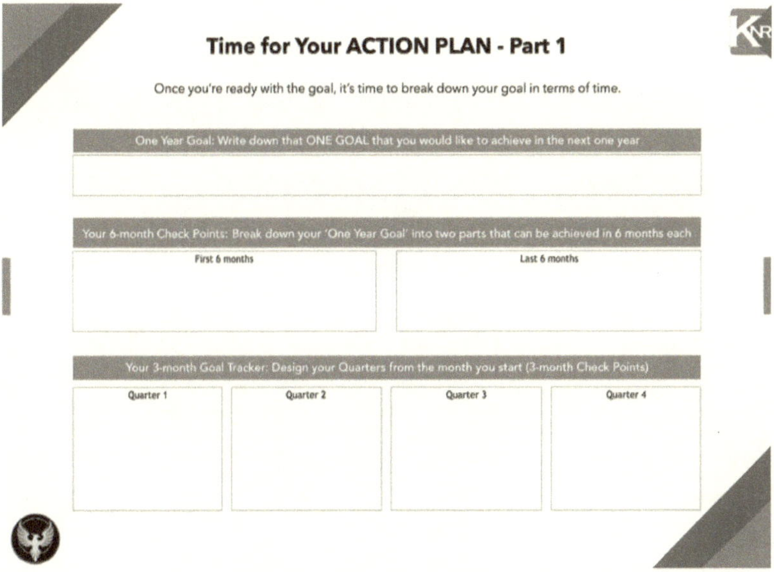

Time for Your ACTION PLAN - Part 1

Once you're ready with the goal, it's time to break down your goal in terms of time.

One Year Goal: Write down that ONE GOAL that you would like to achieve in the next one year

Your 6-month Check Points: Break down your 'One Year Goal' into two parts that can be achieved in 6 months each

First 6 months

Last 6 months

Your 3-month Goal Tracker: Design your Quarters from the month you start (3-month Check Points)

Quarter 1

Quarter 2

Quarter 3

Quarter 4

Image 10:   One Year Action Plan

ONE YEAR Goal:

- Break down your 'One Year Goal' into two parts that can be achieved in 6 months each. Clearly define where is it that you need to be in the next 6 months to reach your 'One Year Goal' by this time next year.

6-month goal:

- Break each 6-month goal into two checkpoints of 3 months each and work on splitting up these 3 months of work further down. This is important to check if you're on track with your 6-month goal, which will eventually play a crucial role by the end of your 'One Year Goal'.

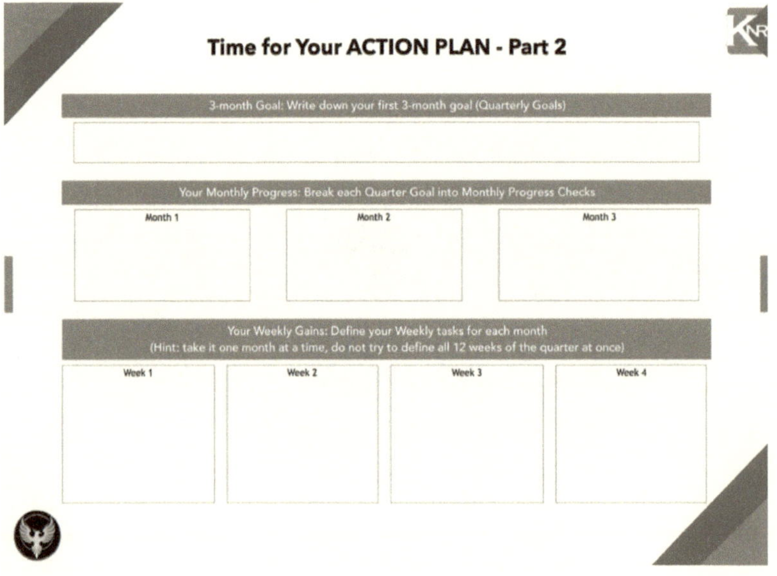

Image 11:   3-month Action Plan

3- month goal:

- Break each 3-month goal into 3 goals of 1 month each, so that you can check your own progress every month and decide where you need to improve and where you can slow down to reach your 'ONE YEAR' goal.

1-month goal:

Break each 1 month's goal into Weekly milestones which would consist of day-to-day planners and journals. Extremely important to know what you would want to achieve in th e next 4 weeks so that you can check your progress by the end of each month.

Weekly milestones:

- Weekly milestones can be broken down into 'Daily Tasks'.

The best part is, that you don't have to define tasks for each day of the week, you can decide if you want to work for one day in the week or 3 days or 5 days and then write up the tasks accordingly to be achieved on the given day of the week.

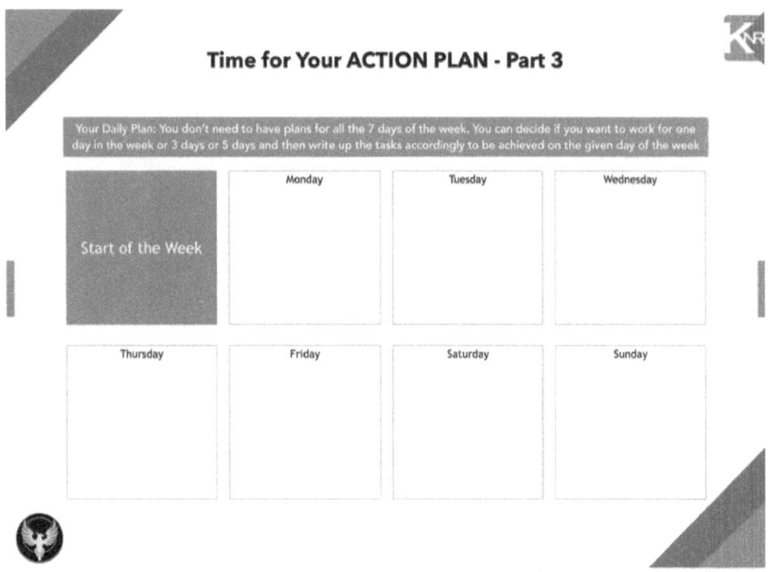

Image 12:   Weekly Milestones Action Plan

You can write down the daily tasks for the week at the beginning of each week, you don't have to write down daily tasks for the entire year, as you might not have a clear idea of what exactly happens in the entire year, so it doesn't make sense. But what you could have an idea about, is how you want to plan this week.

So take some time out every weekend and define your daily tasks for the upcoming week, so that you're clear about what you'll be doing in the next few days.

Now, all that we discussed till now in this activity section is physical work, just process-oriented planning.

But there's another aspect that plays a very important role when it comes to setting and achieving your goals. **THE EMOTIONAL VALUE.**

What is the Emotional Value that you carry, which makes you want to achieve this Goal in the next ONE year? There are 3 questions that you need to answer for yourself before you start working on the action plan for achieving your goals and they're as follows:

- **'WHY'** are you doing this? (What is your Intrinsic Motivation to achieve this goal?)
- What are you **'THINKING'** right now? (What is your Rational thought behind wanting to achieve this goal?)
- What are you **'FEELING'** right now? (What is your Intuition saying about wanting to achieve this goal?)

Answer these 3 questions in all honesty before you start to work on your Action Plan and you'll see the purpose behind willing to put the time and effort to achieve the goal, come to light.

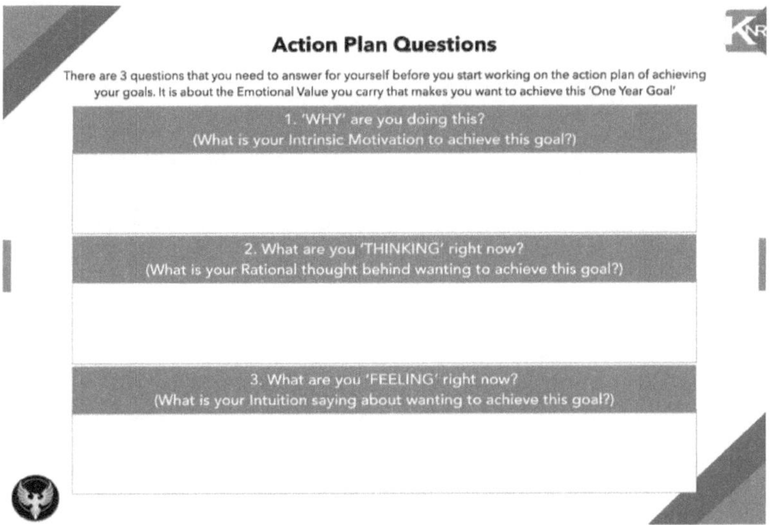

Image 13: Your Emotional Value Questions

The answers to these questions will be your driving force behind reaching your goals at any point in your life. Whenever in doubt, just take a step back and remind yourself of the answers to these questions that made you start your journey towards achieving your goal in the first place. If there's no Emotional Value to your goals, then just the physical planning will not be enough to reach where you want to. So, please keep in mind to remind yourself about the Emotional Value that you carry for achieving your goals.

As in the other sections, you'll find some activity sheets to define your 'Action Plans' and to write down your 'Emotional Value' answers to the 3 important questions regarding your goals.

With a newfound understanding of how to break down your s.m.a.r.t. goals into achievable ACTION PLANS and the reasoning of Your Emotional Value to achieving those goals, let's get into action by answering the questions given above.

Please make use of the templates for your respective answers to keep your progress on track.

See you in the next chapter.

CHAPTER 5

Your Energy Matrix

AN ATTRIBUTION TO YOUR SELF-MOTIVATION

"The quality of your life depends on the quality of your distinctions."

– Thaddeus Lawrence

Is there something called an Energy Matrix? Really?

What is it about anyway?

I know, I know, there might be a lot of questions going on in your head looking at this title, but let's just explore a little more, shall we?

Speaking of YOUR ENERGY, the primary factor that determines the highs and lows of your energy is your INTRINSIC (or SELF) MOTIVATION.

Attribute: SELF MOTIVATION

Being self-motivated consists of enjoying what you do, having an emotional value attached to your goals (the 'WHY?', of your goal-setting), that'll drive you to work towards achieving your goals, and not just being motivated by external factors like money or status

In simpler words, what is it that gives you a 'HIGH' to keep going despite not getting the desired outcome in every situation?

If you can answer the 'WHY?' of your doings, you'll understand the 'WHAT?' of Your BEING.

So it is all about understanding how your personal ENERGIES function and managing them effectively to feel alive all the time. Energy Management might be a common term with respect to your Physical Energy, but sometimes you might hear people complaining that they're mentally drained or emotionally drained.

Where are these coming from?

So to manage your energies effectively, you need to first understand the different kinds of energies that you will have to play with, day-in and day-out.

Your Energy Management System or **'The Energy Matrix'** as I would like to call it, can be classified into 4 types broadly and they are as follows: (in no particular order of priority or importance)

- **Physical Energy:** Defined by the Energy of Your Cognition and Physical Awareness. For you to replenish this energy, you'll need a quick change of your physical state, be it the environment, going for a walk or a jog, or maybe even a quick push-up workout routine can bring you back your energy.
- **Mental Energy:** Defined by the Energy of Your Spontaneity and Focus. For you to replenish this energy, you'll need to have some time for yourself in peace, settle down all your thoughts and then focus on the task at hand. It is very important to stay relaxed and keep calm.

- **Emotional Energy:** Defined by the Energy of Your Emotions and Personal Connections. For you to replenish this energy, you'll need feel the connection in things that you do. It becomes very important for you to feel that the work is YOURS to be done and not doing something for the sake of it.
- **Spiritual Energy:** Defined by the Energy of Your Deliberation and Purpose. For you to replenish this energy, you'll need to feel the intention behind the work. You'll always seek to understand the purpose of things happening with you and around you. If you don't find a purpose and intention behind your work, you tend to lose interest and the energy to carry on.

Understanding the angle from which you innately approach a given situation in your life, determines the kind of energy that powers you or gets drawn out of you in dealing with the situation.

Based on Your Personality and other preferences, different people tend to look at a situation from different angles. These angles are those natural traits that kick in when you are faced with certain problems.

"What are these angles?", I hear you ask.

Well, we can broadly define 4 of these angles which eventually define the quadrants of your natural energy preferences:

1. **The Cognitive Angle** - expending your energy on the knowledge and comprehension of information that you might need in a given situation. This defines your Logical Quadrant which is a combination of the 'Result-oriented & Process-oriented' factors of influence.

Explanation: I call this quadrant, the 'Edison & The Bulb'. As the story goes, Thomas Alva Edison apparently, tried out about 10,000 different elements before discovering that Tungsten is the one that should go on a light bulb for good. Here his hunger for achieving the result was fuelled by his energy for COGNITION (or knowledge).

Is yours too?

2. **The Spontaneous Angle** - expending your energy on intuition or a sudden flash of an idea that you might have in need. This defines your Eurekaaa Moments which is a combination of the 'Result-oriented & Performance-oriented' factors of influence.

Explanation: This quadrant is represented by the theory of 'Newton & The Apple', which famously goes like this; Isaac Newton, who is considered (almost) the father of modern physics, (remembering Newton's 3 Laws of Physics), needed a spark of an apple falling from the tree to get his 'Eurekaaa Moment' of realising there's gravity below his feet which makes things fall down. Fascinating, isn't it?

Do you have YOUR OWN APPLE STORY too?

Feel free to write it in the box below to remind yourself of your SUPERPOWER ;)

3. **The Emotional Angle** - expending your energy on your personal connections and a sense of purpose. Now, this is your Artistic Quadrant which is a combination of the 'People-oriented & Performance-oriented' factors of influence.

Explanation: This is a quadrant which works on your EMOTIONS. You can feel the vibes even before things start to unfold. You would need to get connected to anything you do emotionally so that your work can make sense to you. So your energies in this quadrant depend on the effect of your emotions in a given situation.

Are you CONNECTED to this chapter and my book yet? :P

4. **The Deliberate Angle** - expending your energy on your ability to introspect and the stability of following step-by-step processes. I call this quadrant 'Mindful Flashback', which is defined by the 'Energy of Your Deliberation' (to do things consciously and intentionally). This quadrant is a combination of 'Process-oriented & People-oriented' factors of influence.

Explanation: Represented by the 'A-haa' moments in your life, this is the quadrant that helps you connect with unseen energies that you feel at times. Some may call it '6th sense', others may call it 'Spiritual Energy', but the key to managing your energy in this quadrant is to enable conscious living.

BEING 100% PRESENT WITH WHATEVER YOU'RE DOING and that'll answer the 'WHY?' of your doing.

How DELIBERATE are you at this very moment, reading the book?

Feel Free to Write Your Experiences with Your Energy Matrix

Just to sum things up, we have:

- **The Logical Quadrant** - which corresponds to your 'Physical Energy' defined by your Cognition, where you need some kind of physical activity to boost up your energy (like going for a walk, a jog or a workout)
- **The 'Eurekaaa' Quadrant** - which corresponds to your 'Mental Energy' defined by your Spontaneity, where you would need the right environment to stay calm and focussed (the higher your focus, the better your energy)
- **The Artistic Quadrant** - which corresponds to your 'Emotional Energy' defined by your Emotions, where you would need a personal connection to the things that you would like to do (where there is no will, there is no way you would do it)
- **The 'A-haa' Moments Quadrant** - which corresponds to your 'Spiritual Energy' defined by your Deliberation, where you would need to be present at the moment with your thoughts and yourself to get answers to your questions (nurturing your INTRAPERSONAL abilities to connect to your spiritual dimension)

Hope the Quadrants of Your Energy Matrix make better sense now than when we started this chapter. Your Self Motivation (or Intrinsic Motivation) from understanding the **'WHY?'**'s of your life translates into the kind of energies that can either power you up or bring you down.

In connection to the names of these energies that I have mentioned, I need to take the name of one person who's made a huge impact on my life recently.

The name is **'THADDEUS LAWRENCE'**, my Coach, my Mentor, an amazing Leader and constant support to all of us in his community. He is the founder of 'The Coaching Hand', an amazing community which believes in 'Human Connections' more than anything else. What an inspiration, I tell you. You have to experience his energy at least once in your lifetime. It is only fitting to talk about Thaddeus when we are talking about ENERGIES.

If you know, you know ;)

Why am I mentioning him here?

It is because of my association with him that I understood how to organise and manage my Life in a meaningful way. There is sure a long way to go but I definitely have a guiding light in my life now, which I can follow blindly without giving it a second thought.

Now, the words;

- **Physical Energy**
- **Mental Energy**
- **Emotional Energy**
- **Spiritual Energy**

are borrowed from one of his sessions about managing our energies. The synergies between what I wanted to convey and what he explained in that session were so prominently visible that I couldn't help but adapt some of that content into my theory.

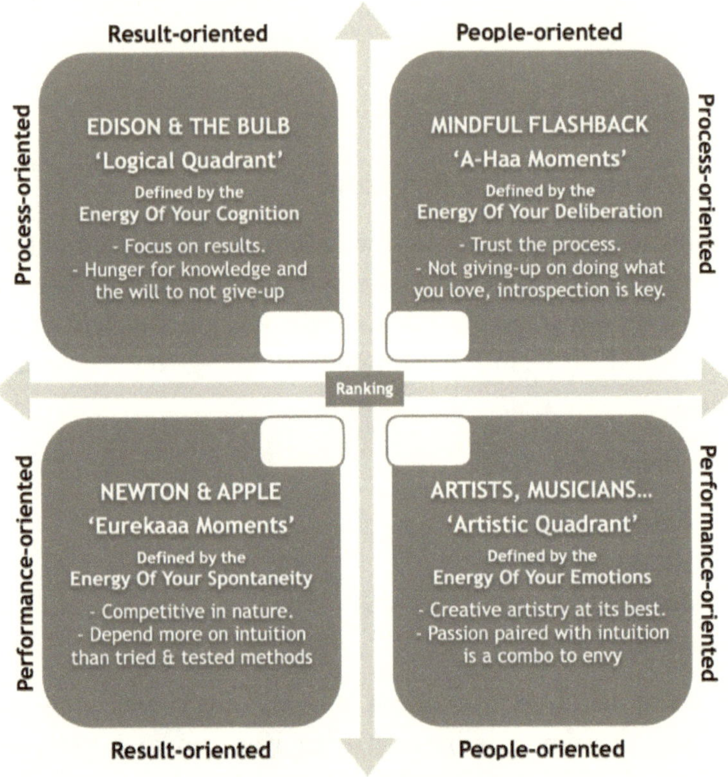

Image 14:   Energy Matrix

Could you rank them from 1 to 4 (1 being the most likely quadrant and 4 being the least), in the image given above?

With that said, we've established in this chapter that, to keep your intrinsic motivation going, the 'WHY?' of what you do plays a major role. To keep Your Energies HIGH and keep going, to learn to replenish Your Energies in situations that don't go your way, answers to your 'WHY?', become very important.

With that in mind, now it's time to move on to the next activity which is rather interesting.

Read on to find out.

The Section Coming Up...

On the note of answering the 'WHY?'s of our being, let's do a bit of 'Visualization' in the next section. It is called, 'The Year in Your Life'. It is a technique where you shift the focus from your current location (Reality) to the desired destination (Results), where you see yourself being successful.

Ready to do some time travelling?

Hop on board and let's fly through time in the next section.

See you on the other side of your space-time travel. Have fun.

ACTIVITY SECTION 5: THE YEAR IN YOUR LIFE

Hello!

Welcome back. It's great to see you here.

Hope you had a productive time understanding your emotional side of the goals you set for yourself and working out an action plan to start working towards your goals.

If you haven't completed the previous activity, please do it before you go ahead with this video, it'll help in being a little clearer in your thoughts.

And now, time for some 'Visualisation & Imagination'.

Unlike the other activities where you had to use your brain to do some physical work, here we'll only use your mind to do some intangible work.

Please make sure that you're in a quiet place before you start this activity so that there's not much disturbance when you're thinking or visualising things.

Don't worry it's a fairly simple exercise and you just need to be aware of what you're thinking and feeling as long as you are into visualising.

So let's get started, shall we?

To begin with, there are a few things you need to do. So far, we've done two assessments of self, and answered a few questions on setting S.M.A.R.T. goals.

Now, please bring all the completed sheets of 'Wheel of Life', 'S.M.A.R.T. Goals', and 'EI Competency Assessment' and place them in front of you (if you are currently reading on an electronic device, please write your results down on a sheet of paper and keep it in front of you), so that you can see the results of these three sheets.

Hope you've been honest in your answers because remember, you're doing this to understand yourself better and not to impress anyone. OK?

Now you know where you stand right now based on your answers in all the three sheets in front of you. Just glance through the assessments and your answers once again just in case you don't remember. Take a deep breath (inhaaaaaale & exhaaaaaale) and try to picture your 'Wheel of Life' graph on the wall in front of you. Can you picture it on the wall?

Once you have a visual picture of it, I want you to think about your score on the 'EI Competency Assessment' which was out of 120, also on the same wall.

Remind yourself of the skills with the lowest scores and those with the highest scores that added up to your total EI Competency score. Done?

Now, think of your S.M.A.R.T. goal that you would like to achieve in the next one year.

Take your time, there's no hurry, in case you need more time to think about your goal, you can always go back to that activity section, think about it and then come back to work on this section. It can be a small goal, which you know is achievable, that you can measure when you achieve it. You don't have to think of an outrageous goal that you want to achieve by next year.

We're just starting and let's start small, once you get a hang of this process and technique, then you can think of bigger, ambitious goals.

Imagine a picture of what you want to achieve a year from now, and mentally put that visual on the same wall, along with your Wheel of Life and EI Competency score.

Ok, so do we have the picture of your 'Wheel of Life' graph, your 'EI Competency Assessment' score and your S.M.A.R.T. goal that you would like to achieve by this time next year?

Great, now let's do some time travelling. Whatever day of the year it is today, imagine you travelling to next year, same day. For example, if today is 25 January 2023, I'll need you to imagine that you travel a year ahead of where you are, that is to 25 January 2024. Ok?

Your Life in 2024...

Time to VISUALISE. Take a deep breath and Visualise the following.

Life is great, YOU HAVE ACHIEVED THE GOAL that you had set a year ago and you're looking forward to new challenges that life throws at you. Take your time, there's no need to be in a hurry. Take enough time to get a clear picture of your successful life in the year 2024.

Now, visualise your 'Wheel of Life' graph on the day you achieve your S.M.A.R.T. goal. Again no hurry, take your time and observe what has changed in your Wheel of Life graph from 2023 to 2024.

Is it better in the areas that needed improvement or are they still the same? What's the improvement that you can see?

Once you visualise the new improved graph, let's look at your EI Competency score on the day you achieve your S.M.A.R.T. goal. Take your time and visualise the number that can justify you having a successful year. Done?

Is your score better than what it was a year ago? Which skill have you improved upon and what aspect of your Emotional Intelligence has made the difference to improve your EI score over last year's score?

Now replace your old visuals on the wall with these new improved visuals;

- Achieving your S.M.A.R.T. goal
- Improved Wheel of Life graph
- Improved EI competency score

How does it look now? Does that make you feel happy?

Well, you can close your eyes now and cherish the moment for a while. If you are feeling happy, let the feeling sink in completely into you. Stay in the moment of your new achievement and a brand new state of BEING. This is the NEW YOU.

Wonderful, thank you so much for participating in this Visualising Technique, give yourself a pat on the back for the great work done first.

Now, in the space provided on the next page, write down the S.M.A.R.T. goal that you achieved in your visualisation by the same time, next year. Also, draw a spider graph of your new improved 'Wheel of Life' and your new improved 'EI Competency' score, in the respective spaces provided.

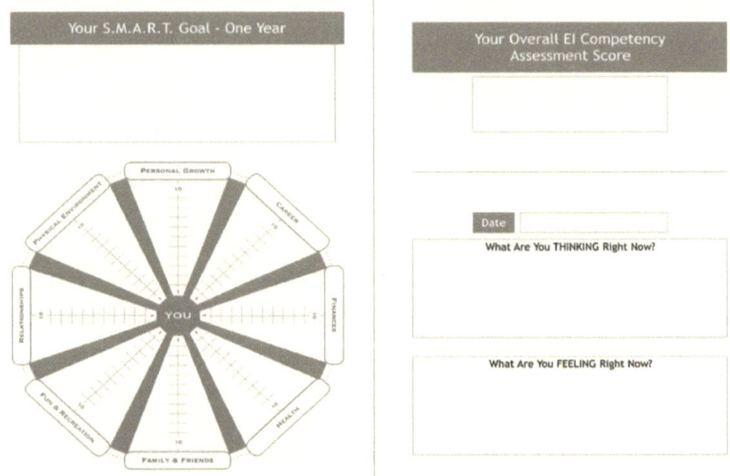

Image 15:   Visualising the Year in Your Life

Now to the most important part, journal your thoughts and feelings right now. In the right-bottom half of the activity sheet given, write down today's date and record 'What you're feeling right now' And 'What you're thinking right now', regarding your goals and competencies.

One important thing that you need to understand is the reason behind this exercise, it's not just for fun but also an amazing technique for you to be with yourself for some time and focus on your feelings and thoughts.

Journaling your thoughts and feelings frequently, improves your relationship with yourself and trust me, that's one thing which is becoming exceedingly negligent but extremely important in our busy world. Take some time out every day if possible and think about what has been your relationship with yourself today.

That question is powerful and your answers to it every day, can transform the way you think and feel about yourself.

Become more aware and conscious of yourself.

And that's the foundation for Self-awareness and building your life around the understanding of yourself, your abilities, your strengths and limitations.

In case you could not figure out any of the three aspects that you visualised through this process, don't worry, you can go through this activity any number of times you want to, and for multiple goals as well, but keep it one goal at a time so that you can feel confident enough in achieving your goals.

I know you had to read through to get this activity done today, but once you are familiar with the concept and the script of this technique, you can do it with your eyes closed. Not having to read through the script, and that way it would be more effective.

The more you practice this 'Visualisation' technique, the more confidence you tend to build on your abilities and competencies in the long run. So please do practice it often. It's not a do-it-once and miracles happen kind of thing. Do it once and keep it going at least once a week. **Manifest your Visualisation.**

There's one request from my end though, whatever you do through the process, the goals, visualisations, imaginations, please do it honestly and diligently. Remember, this is for you to become more aware of yourself, not to impress anybody.

So, hope you enjoyed doing some Visualisations and Imagination. I sincerely hope you really get whatever you positively visualised achieving by this time next year and continue growing with many more results coming your way. With that, we'll conclude this section. **Remember, this need not be a one-time thing, you can come back to this exercise whenever you are in doubt or not feeling very confident.**

See you in the next chapter.

CHAPTER 6

Your Communication Preference

AN ATTRIBUTION TO YOUR EMPATHY

"The way we communicate with others and with ourselves ultimately determines the quality of our lives."

– Tony Robbins

Before we get into the nuances of communication, let's try to shed some light on the concept of EMPATHY, shall we?

Empathy by definition is the ability to understand the other person's emotional response in a given situation. This is only possible when one has achieved self-awareness—as one cannot understand others until he understands himself.

Communication is not just about talking the way you know. It has more to do with understanding how the other person perceives the messages that you intend to convey.

Attribute: EMPATHY

To be empathetic means that you are able to identify and understand others' emotions i.e. imagining yourself in someone else's position.

When there's no proper understanding of the communication channel, do you know what the result is?

MIS-COMMUNICATION.

One of the primary reasons for most of your mishaps in life is Miscommunication.

It is either you don't understand 'HOW' to convey a message to your audience or the other person doesn't understand 'HOW' you prefer messages to be conveyed. Or even worse, both.

REMEMBER: It is not always about what you convey that matters, it is more about HOW you convey it. The tone of your communication matters too. And I mean 'A LOT'.

And to know, HOW your messages can be conveyed, you need to understand the different types of communicators that exist. So here we go.

Broadly divided into 4 categories, the different types of communicators are:

1. **Analytical Communicators** - who emphasise LOGIC and INTEGRITY OF DATA
2. **Intuitive Communicators** - who emphasise OPTIMISTIC ENERGY and POSITIVITY
3. **Personal Communicators** - who emphasise EMOTIONAL CONNECTIONS and SENSIBILITY
4. **Functional Communicators** - who emphasise STABILITY and ACCOUNTABILITY

Each of these types of communicators speaks a different 'HOW' Language. For you to have effective communication with any of these types of communicators, you need to understand the aspects to emphasise, more than just talking out the matter.

Now let's explore the communication quadrants, in a little more detail as shown in the image below:

- **Analytical communication:** The essence of this quadrant is having strong dominance towards Written Communication. These communicators prefer to 'Bring the Numbers' on their table when they communicate. This quadrant is formed by the combination of Result-oriented & Process-oriented factors of influence, hence the focus on 'Data & Logic'.

- **Intuitive communication:** This is a quadrant where you would have a stronger dominance for Pictorial Communication. These communicators prefer keeping the conversations 'Short & Sweet' and conveying their messages in an aesthetically pleasing manner. The Intuitive quadrant is formed by the combination of Performance-oriented & Result-oriented factors of influence, hence the emphasis on 'Positivity & Optimistic Energy'

- **Personal communication:** Personal communication is about having a stronger urge to feel an emotional connection when you speak or convey a message. People with a stronger dominance in this quadrant would prefer Non-verbal communication as their primary means of conveying messages. It can be through actions or expressions, they would bring out their emotions in more ways than just words. They prefer to 'Open up'. The combination of People-oriented & Performance-oriented factors of influence ensures that these people don't hurt others either by their words or actions. Hence the emphasis on their 'Emotional Connections & Sensibilities'.

- **Functional communication:** This quadrant is all about the 'matter-of-fact' way you communicate or handle things with people. These communicators would build a strong sense of Verbal communication and they prefer talking point-to-point. This quadrant is formed by the combination of Process-oriented & People-oriented factors of influence. Hence the emphasis on 'Accountability & Stability' of their conversations and so they would trust only those people who're thorough with the details of their 'Whole Picture Ideas'.

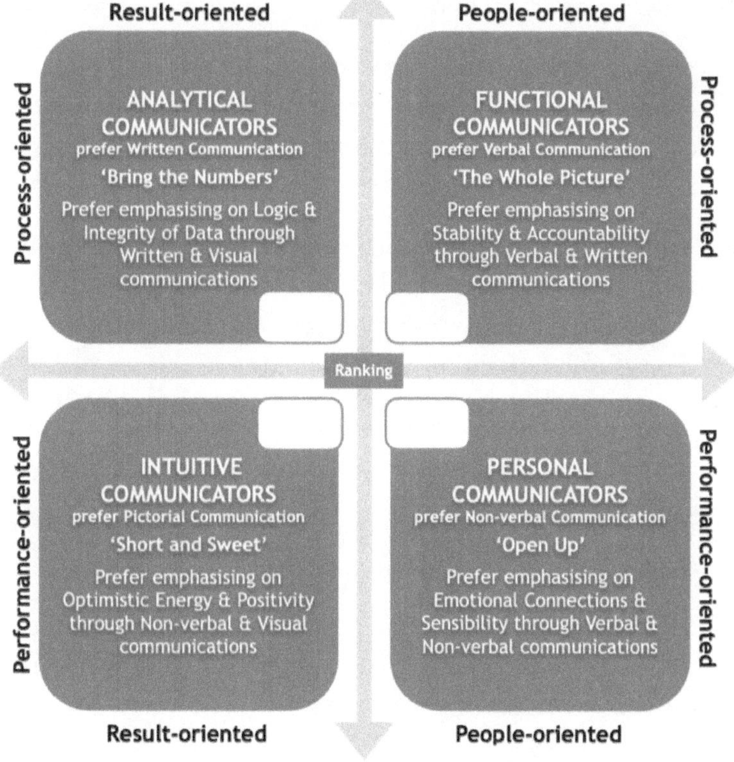

Image 16:   Clarity in Communication

Having said that, which of these quadrants do you think you communicate from the most?

Can you rank your preference of communication from 1 to 4 (1 being your most favourable quadrant and 4 being your least favourable)?

It is not just about your natural inclination towards a particular quadrant to keep in mind while you communicate, but also the natural inclination of your audience.

You need to understand what quadrant the other person is communicating from, to deliver your message more effectively.

Once you understand each other's dominant quadrants of communication, your conversations start to flow more meaningfully, thus taking out the possibilities of miscommunication to a great extent.

We humans, as a species, rely on good communication more than any other creature in the world because of our varied sensibilities and our ability to think (mostly overthink), we interpret things based on the understanding of our worlds.

The point is, that conveying a message to your fellow human is not as simple as asking your pet to 'Sit' or 'Fetch'.

It's a lot more complicated and out of this complexity is where the chaos of misunderstandings happens.

When you are responsible enough to respect the sensibilities of people around you, sooner or later, those very people will learn to respect your sensibilities too.

Hence, a better understanding of intentions can be formed, resulting in more meaningful communications.

Remember what I mentioned at the beginning of this chapter?

Communication is not just about talking the way you know, it is always a two-way process.

Things have to be conveyed and received on the same level for them to be meaningful. If not, you're just asking for trouble.

And that's been a bigger problem with most of us in recent times because nobody has the patience to listen to the other person from a different point of view. It is always 'my opinion' and 'my point' that matters to everybody.

Respect the fact that **information exchange** is a two-way street and give it enough space for the other person to travel, then you'll see for yourself that the number of accidents happening in your journey would go down drastically.

Pro Tip: Listen more than you speak. That's a GOLDEN RULE of any successful Communication.

That's enough food for thought on having a 'Clarity in Communication'.

That's all for now. Hope you have a great time exploring the different types of communicators in your life and enjoy your newfound key to Effective Communications.

The Section Coming Up...

Let's try and develop a Daily Routine of Planning and Journaling our days so that we can be more aware and conscious of 'what we do?' and 'why we do?' things.

In the next section, I'll take you through a simple template to follow a routine of Daily Planning and Journaling which, when practised consistently would help you build discipline and confidence in yourself.

So, let's get started.

ACTIVITY SECTION 6: PLANNING & JOURNALING YOUR DAY

What is Planning Your Day?
Why is Journaling Your Day important?

Short Answer, **To develop self-discipline and build self-confidence.**

How does a simple task like Planning your day and journaling your experiences make such a huge impact to develop discipline and confidence, you ask?

It is all about developing consistency daily in what you do. A DAILY ROUTINE, if you may.

My coach always says, "If you are CONSISTENT with Your Actions, Results will Appear." -- Thaddeus Lawrence, Lead Coach & Trainer at The Coaching Hand.

(Pssst.. if you have not heard of this man yet, well YOU SHOULD..! Period. Go Google NOW)

Coming back to the topic, developing a Daily Routine helps you be CONSISTENT with your Actions, which in turn get you Results. Sounds SIMPLE, doesn't it?

Am I hearing you ask, IS IT EASY?

Well, that's the catch, 'Simple things are seldom the easy ones.'

The actual difficulty is not in doing those EASY things, but in maintaining to do the same things day after day.

Let's look at the image given below, it is a simple one-page template to;

Begin your day with:

- A Daily Affirmation
- Plan Your Day with Top 3 Priorities for Work, Family & Self-care

End your day by:

- Rating Your Day for Satisfaction in terms of Work, Family & Self-care before you go to sleep
- Journaling Your Thoughts by answering the given questions

If you can make it a routine to follow this template daily, you'll see a shift in your BEING even before you know it.

Does that sound simple enough to follow now?

Here's the template that you need to follow to build a routine of 'Planning & Journaling'.

PLAN YOUR DAY AND JOURNAL YOUR THOUGHTS

BEGINNING MY DAY WITH A DAILY AFFIRMATION

MY TOP 3 PRIORITIES FOR THE DAY

TOP 3 WORK TASKS

TOP 3 FAMILY TASKS

TOP 3 SELF-CARE TASKS

ENDING THE DAY BY JOURNALING MY THOUGHTS

RATE YOUR DAY   Work ☆☆☆☆☆   Family ☆☆☆☆☆   Self-care ☆☆☆☆☆

HIGHLIGHTS OF THE DAY

HOW COULD I HAVE MADE IT BETTER?

TODAY I AM GRATEFUL FOR?

Image 17:   Daily Planner & Journal

I have made the template as simple as possible for you to make it a habit easily and not have to spend too much time on it. Please be consistent.

As James Clear mentions in his book 'Atomic Habits', "Success is the product of daily habits—not once-in-a-lifetime transformations."

Planning & Journaling your days is one of the most effective ways to organise the way you live your life. And when you are consistent in organising the days of your life, you'll eventually end up being more productive, satisfied and a couple of steps ahead of most others who choose to stay back.

Now it is up to you to decide if you want to be with a flock that complains and doesn't move or with a flock that makes things happen. The choice will always be yours. So you better choose your actions wisely.

Remember: Consistent Actions always lead to Commendable Results.

On that note, I would like to inform you that this is officially the last activity section of this book. Hope you had a great time 'Introducing You to Yourself' through this book.

I am truly GRATEFUL that you decided to get a copy of my first ever book in your hands. I wouldn't claim that this experience would change your life but it is definitely a beginning towards 'Your Journey of Self-Clarity'.

Thank you so much for being a part of this journey with me in 'Introducing You to Yourself'.

Hope to see you again soon, where I wish to introduce you to the art of Fingerprint Analysis.

I am super excited to bring you the concepts of Fingerprints and their importance in your life that you wouldn't have been aware of. They are more important than you could ever think, so get ready to venture into the exciting WORLD of FINGERPRINTS in my next book;

'Introducing You to Your Fingerprints'.

Till then, have a great time with all the activities provided in this book. Feel free to go through each of them as many times as you like. And yes, please make sure you develop a daily routine of Planning & Journaling your days. That's VERY IMPORTANT.

With that said, it is time to say Goodbye for now.

See you in the next book. Take care and stay safe.